John A. Haddock

The Routes Pursued by the Excursion Steamers upon the St. Lawrence River

From Clayton and Gananoque to Westminster Park and Alexandria Bay

John A. Haddock

The Routes Pursued by the Excursion Steamers upon the St. Lawrence River
From Clayton and Gananoque to Westminster Park and Alexandria Bay

ISBN/EAN: 9783337145156

Printed in Europe, USA, Canada, Australia, Japan

Cover: Foto ©Andreas Hilbeck / pixelio.de

More available books at **www.hansebooks.com**

THE ROUTES

PURSUED BY

THE EXCURSION STEAMERS

UPON THE

ST. LAWRENCE RIVER

FROM

*CLAYTON AND GANANOQUE TO WESTMINSTER
PARK AND ALEXANDRIA BAY*

PUBLISHED BY
JNO. A. HADDOCK AND J. H. DURHAM
CLAYTON AND ALEXANDRIA BAY, N. Y.

PRINTED AND BOUND BY
WEED-PARSONS PRINTING COMPANY
ALBANY, N. Y.

COPYRIGHTED, 1895.
All rights reserved.

To the Rambler.

THIS little book is not written with the idea that it will take the place of more pretentious guide books, nor as a history of The Thousand Islands of the St. Lawrence River; nor yet is it written especially in the interest of any steamboat company, nor of any particular route; but solely to point out to the visitor such places of interest among the islands as are most worthy of attention, and the means by which they may be reached. In addition, what may be termed side routes or excursions have been pointed out, which if taken will add largely to the interest of a summer tour in and around the St. Lawrence River region.

Believing, also, that incidents which have occurred so long ago among and in the vicinity of the Thousand Islands as to have become history, will add much to its interest, a brief sketch of each is reproduced, and the locality in which it took place pointed out.

The writer claims no originality in these sketches. They have been drawn from the best attainable sources, re-written and condensed to suit the scope of the work, and the only merit the writer can claim, is, that he has been diligent in his researches, and in conse-

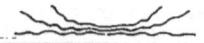

King · Joseph's · Hermitage.

A charming resort, just completed and open to guests, only one-quarter of a mile from the Carthage and Adirondack line, from whence two daily trains connect with the R., W. & O. system, at Carthage, seventeen miles distant.

This Hotel commands a full view of lovely Lake Bonaparte and is connected with woodland scenery of inexpressible charm, once a part of the vast territory owned by Joseph Bonaparte in Northern New York. The ex-king had selected this ground as his hunting headquarters, and was heard to speak of its loveliness and beauty, and with a view to perpetuate this interesting and historical fact this resort has been so named.

Summer guests at the St. Lawrence River would enjoy as a matter of diversion a short stay at King Joseph's Hermitage. Guest will receive most genteel treatment at fair rates. For information address

JOSEPH PAHUD, Prop.,
Harrisville, N. Y.

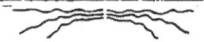

quence has brought to light some interesting events which have escaped the scrutiny of those who have gleaned in the same field. If, therefore, through the perusal of this little manual the reader has added to the enjoyment of a sojourn among, or a visit to, The Thousand Islands, or if it has in any degree increased the pleasure and satisfaction of an Island Ramble, or augmented his stock of knowledge, the object of the work is accomplished.

The truth is, that in these Island Rambles there is something more than sensuous enjoyment. They transport one to a higher plane. They are, in a large sense, refining. They develop a love for the beautiful in nature. They are, in short, promoters of a true æstheticism. They educate, they expand, they exalt. Those who look often upon these scenes assimilate, unconsciously though it may be, many of their beauties until reaching a higher standpoint with a broader view, they

"* * * Take no private road,
But look through Nature up to Nature's God."

Having thus, dear Rambler, set forth the "ends and aims" of this little book, the writer leaves it in your hands, with the earnest hope that it may answer every purpose for which it was originally designed

Cornwall Brothers,

TICKET AGENTS,

And General Dealers in

Dry Goods, Notions, Groceries,

CROCKERY, CLOTHING, ETC.

CAMP AND ISLAND SUPPLIES A SPECIALTY.

Also Agents for Huyler's Candies.   ALEXANDRIA BAY, N. Y.

The Rambles

IN taking the rambles among the islands the visitor must be governed by his or her own convenience as to time. The steamer ISLANDER makes the most interesting trip, and the longest; its distance being in fact nearer sixty miles than the usually advertised fifty-mile ramble. In so doing the ISLANDER visits some localities of great interest, where other excursion boats are unable to go, owing to a greater draught of water. This is again alluded to under another head. All these facts are set forth in the bills provided, and put into the hands of an efficient and gentlemanly corps of advertising agents. On every trip among the islands a special agent accompanies the boat, who will point out every spot of interest, thereby largely increasing the pleasures of the occasion.

If at any time, however, a special route is to be taken, or the managers have decided upon an extra trip having some special attraction, you may rest assured that it will be duly advertised and set forth; and when such a trip is proclaimed, don't fail to examine this little Manual carefully; because it is very likely that if the trip is within the scope of a fifty-mile ramble, it will give you some

W. G. CHAFFEE,
Oswego, N. Y.

TEACHES . . . .

Shorthand,

Typewriting,

∴ *Penmanship,*

Bookkeeping ∴

∴ *and Spanish.*

GOOD POSITIONS By Mail or Personally, and Secures for all his Shorthand . . . . Pupils when Competent.

AGENT FOR THE

CALIGRAPH,
the best Typewriter, and for the

MIMEOGRAPH,
the best Duplicator.

Stenographers Furnished Business Men without charge for my Services. Correspondence Solicited. Circulars Free.

W. G. CHAFFEE,
OSWEGO, N. Y.

interesting information in advance. In order to a clear comprehension of the sights and scenes among the Islands, let us take an afternoon ramble, and close the day with a grand Search Light Excursion at night on the noble steamer St. Lawrence, as a finishing touch, a fitting complement, a rounding out to the ramble of the day.

We have all either seen or heard of those wonderful dioramic paintings, in which is portrayed a lovely landscape with wooded hills, turreted towers, flowing streams and falling cataracts, which, under the marvelous light of a spring morning, seem a veritable reality. Suddenly the scene changes; night approaches; day-light gradually disappears, and the soft May moon lights the landscape; every harsh and rugged line is smoothed away, while the deep shadows lurk in leafy coverts; lights sparkle and gleam from castle and tower; the streams become threads of molten silver, and the cataracts draperies of filmy lace laden with pearls. I have no fitting language in which to describe the beauty of it all, but far and away above these, a daylight and Search Light ramble, taken as a whole, among the Thousand Islands of the St. Lawrence river, constitute Nature's Great Diorama, elsewhere unequaled on the face of the globe. Even the writer of the book of Job, incomparable in poetic description, having seen these sights, might have written:—

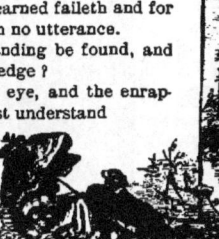

Who, then, shall describe the beauties thereof?
Behold! The language of the learned faileth and for his dreams the poet findeth no utterance.
Where, then, shall the understanding be found, and where is the key of Knowledge?
Look thou upon the brightening eye, and the enraptured look, and thou may'st understand
That voiceless look is eloquence itself.
And from it learn thou, that, like the "Music of the Spheres,"
The language of the soul hath no words

FRONTENAC HOTEL, ROUND ISLAND.

The Frontenac, Round Island, 1000 Islands.

The cuisine and service excellent.
Every room commands a river view.
Electric bells and steam heat.
Pure water from an artesian well.
Kapps' noted orchestra.

Invigorating and healthful qualities of the atmosphere.
No flies or mosquitoes.
Boating, fishing, bowling, billiards and tennis are among the attractions.

E. D. DICKINSON, MANAGER.

ISLANDS IN AMERICAN WATERS, SOUTH OF WESTMINSTER PARK. ALEXANDRIA BAY IN THE DISTANCE.

The Grand Ramble.

Fifty Miles of Gorgeous Scenery.

SWINGING away from the Railway Wharf, at Clayton, where the great New York Central System discharges its thousands of eager sightseers, the steamer Islander, of the Thousand Island Steamboat Company, begins her magnificent ramble among the famous island group. We touch for a moment at the wharf of Round Island Park, with its magnificent Hotel Frontenac as a fit centerpiece for its coastline fringe of elegant cottages. You will probably visit the " Frontenac," and when there, if you desire it, the clerk will furnish you with a list of cottage-owners, so that it is not necessary to take up our space with the list. " Round Island Park " is one of the most delightful resorts among the islands, and will well repay an extended visit. On our left is "Little Round Island," and beyond that lies Colborne's Island, Bluff, Jefferson, Maple and Robbins' Islands

Thousand Island House.

Cor. of Ontario and Brock Sts., KINGSTON, ONT.

CON. MILLAN, Proprietor.

Commodious, Comfortable, Reasonable in Price.

Nearest all the Landings for Steamers, and not ten rods from R. R. Depot.

Fronts the Great City Hall. Open Day and Night.

Information cheerfully given.

In the midst of the Hunting and Fishing Grounds of the Upper St. Lawrence.

There was a tragedy on Maple Island in 1865, a very mysterious one; and it is only within two or three years that any clue to the mystery has been found, and even now, though circumstances seem to point out a reasonable solution, the evidence is incomplete, and in all probability the real facts in the case will never be brought to light. I have only space here to give you a brief outline of the main facts, referring you to Major John A. Haddock's "International Souvenir History of the Thousand Islands," where you will find full and complete —

The Mystery of Maple Island.

In the summer of 1865, in the early part of June, a stranger arrived at the hotel at Fisher's Landing, then kept by John Keech. He was from Gananoque, and had been brought over in a skiff by a well-known oarsman of that village, since deceased. For a few days the stranger contented himself at the hotel, or took short walks into the country, going at one time as far as Omar, a pleasant hamlet about a mile and a half from the Landing, or else, hiring a skiff, he would take a day and row about among the islands.

Finally he one day announced his intention to have a cabin built on one of the islands, the better to enable him to enjoy the pastimes of fishing and hunting, of which he seemed to be extremely fond. Acting on this idea, he hired carpenters, procured lumber, bought a skiff with all its accessories, and all the necessary table furniture and cooking utensils to enable him to "keep house," and "moved" into his new domicile, which was built by the side of a precipice, and so hidden by a thick undergrowth that it could not be seen from a passing skiff. He purchased his supplies from the farmers on a neighboring island, and having books and a violin, for he is said to have been quite a musician, time seemed to slip pleasantly away, though he admitted no one to anything like terms of familiarity, nor invited any guests to his cabin. It may be well to say, in passing, that he was a man seemingly about thirty years of age, black hair and eyes and black chin whiskers, well dressed, very uncommunicative, dark as a Spaniard, and very restless. He had plenty of money, and paid his bills promptly in English gold. The summer passed quietly away, and but for another occurrence, the "Hermit," as people began to speak of him, would have been almost forgotten.

A. C. McINTYRE,

THE

Veteran Photographer

OF THE THOUSAND ISLANDS

ESTABLISHED 1871.

THOUSANDS OF VIEWS.
LARGEST CAMERA IN
NORTHERN NEW YORK.

LIFE-LONG EXPERIENCE.
PRICES REASONABLE.

One night a light was seen on Maple Island, and the conclusion was that the hermit's cabin had caught fire; but not thinking of any personal danger to him, no especial attention was paid to it. It was thought, of course, that he would take his boat and go ashore somewhere, either to Clayton, Grinnell's, or Fisher's Landing; but as he did not put in an appearance anywhere the next morning, a couple of fishermen went ashore on Maple Island, and there they found his dead body. His throat was cut, and on his naked breast there were three crosses slashed with a knife, the crosses being disposed in the form of a triangle.

For a week before this tragedy, several men who, by their language and appearance were set down as Southerners, were quartered at different hotels in Clayton; but on that evening they had settled their bills, and hired some oarsmen to take them to Alexandria Bay, which they did. It was learned later on that they did not stay at Alexandria Bay that night, but no one seemed to know when they left, nor where they went. These facts were brought out on the inquest which was held, but nothing more was discovered at that time. A brief article in the Clayton paper, *On the St. Lawrence*, gave the above facts in substance, and from that slight clue the mystery is well nigh cleared up. As a starting point, the reader may understand that the "three crosses," cut in the form of a triangle, were a well-known sign of a secret society which flourished during the war, both North and South, commonly known as the "Knights of the Golden Circle;" and hence it is fair to presume that the assassins were brother "Knights" of the hermit, who were fulfilling their oaths by murdering him. The next question arose, why should they murder him? What was the cause?

To make this story short I will just say, that certain parties were offered the sum of $300,000 in gold to assassinate Lincoln, Seward, Johnson, Grant, Sherman, Sheridan and one or two other members of the cabinet, and a proportionate sum for as many as were assassinated. There was paid to John H. Surratt, in the Queen's Hotel in Toronto, $100,000 of this sum in English gold, paid to him by the notorious Jake Thompson, at that time an agent for the Confederacy in Canada. There was with John H. Surratt, at the time, John A. Payne, brother to the Payne who was hanged for the attempted assassination of Secretary Seward and his son. John A. Payne was the treasurer of a secret society in Washington; Surratt and Payne

THE NEW WINDSOR,
CLAYTON, N. Y.

A NEW HOUSE.
    CENTRAL LOCATION.
        EVERY CONVENIENCE.
PRICES REASONABLE.
    FRONTING THE GREAT RIVER.
        CUISINE SUPERIOR.

LINLITHGOW.

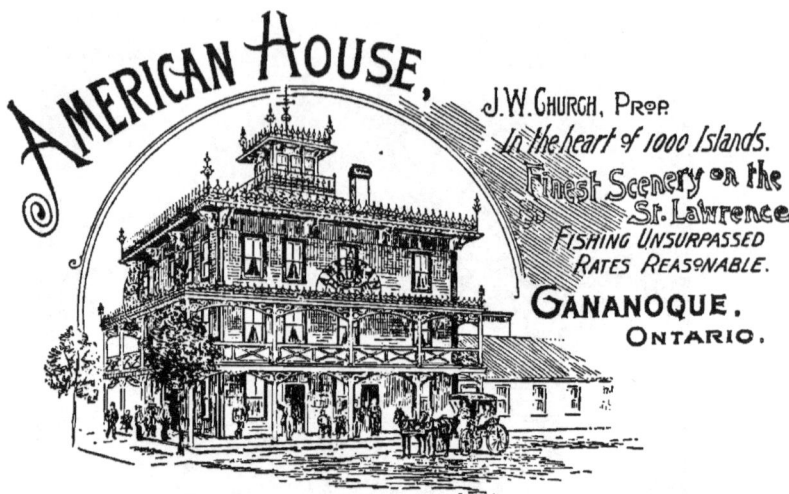

The above Hotel has been newly fitted and furnished throughout for the season of 1895. Its rooms are large and commodious, well furnished, the best of beds, excellent ventilation—in short, ideal rooms. The table is kept supplied with all the delicacies of the season, well cooked, with good service. The bar is supplied with all the best brands of Wines and Liquors, and the best Imported Cigars. The House is but two minutes' walk from the Steamboat Landing, and one minute's walk from the Depot. Terms very reasonable. Special rates on application.

TAKE NOTICE.

When you leave the Steamer Landing, take the first crossing to the right hand side of the street, and the first Hotel is the AMERICAN. Don't forget it. The best House in every respect in Gananoque

Best Oarsmen and Guides on the river provided.

left Toronto the very night the money was paid into Surratt's hands. We all know what became of Surratt, but what of Payne? All the evidences, circumstantial though they be, point to the fact that John A. Payne was murdered on Maple Island, in the St. Lawrence river, by his brother Knights of the Golden Circle, because he failed to divide with them the blood money received for the assassination of Abraham Lincoln. I have no time nor space here to enter into all the facts, but when you have read in the Souvenir all the evidences which have been unearthed, you will agree with the above statement.

We now steam away toward "Grinnell's Island" and the Pullman House landing. Do not make the mistake that some do, and imagine this to be the celebrated Pullman Cottage, because it isn't; but it is one of the very pleasant summer hotels on the river, and lately enlarged one-third in size. Glance along that narrow channel away to our left. It leads past the "Palisades," a huge granite precipice on the head of Wellesley Island, and out into "Eel Bay," and through it a steamer plies her route every two hours to Grand View Park, a beautiful place next to the Canadian channel. Down yonder, in the very narrowest part of the strait, between the "Palisades" and "Murray Island," there was quite a spirited naval battle fought once, the history of which is as follows:

Naval Skirmish on the St. Lawrence.

On the 9th of August, 1813, the schooners Julia and Growler, becoming separated from the remainder of Commodore Chauncey's fleet, set sail down the lake, hotly pursued by several of the English vessels. The Growler succeeded in making the harbor of Oswego, and anchored under the protection of the guns of the fort. The Julia held her course down the lake, with a fair wind, and being a fast sailer, she soon outstripped the English vessels, two of which, the Seneca and Simcoe, had been in close pursuit. The Julia was in command of Mr. Trant, the sailing master, and was armed with one long 32-pounder on a pivot, two long sixes, and forty men. The Simcoe's armament consisted of twelve guns and seventy-six men, and the Seneca's, four guns and forty men. Passing down the river until opposite French creek, Mr. Trant directed his course across the river through what is now known as "Robbins' Cut," the route taken by the splendid St. Lawrence on her search-light excursions between

Capt. SIMEON G. JOHNSON,

PROPRIETOR

Steamer ∵ Nightingale,

AND OF

The Clayton Shipyard.

The Nightingale is a 95-foot Steam Propeller, making six trips each day on week days, and two trips on Sunday, between Clayton and Fine View, stopping each way at Round Island, Pullman's (Grand View Park) and Thousand Island Park.

AN EXCELLENT BOAT, CAREFULLY MANAGED.

Robbins' and Grindstone islands, and out into Eel bay. Here he lay-to near the group of barren rocks known as "Indian Islands," just off Grand View Park. It was not long before his pursuers appeared, reinforced by another small vessel, whose name is not known. The Simcoe and the strange vessel entered the bay from the Canadian channel, while the Seneca had followed the Julia directly through Robbins' cut. For a few moments all was hurry and bustle on board the little schooner. Every sheet that would draw was set, and she sped away for the narrow passage between Wellesley and Hemlock islands, and taking up her position just off the Palisades where the channel begins to widen, she lowered her sails and the crew went to quarters. The enemy came gallantly on with a strong breeze, which increased in force as it sucked through the narrow passage, making it very difficult to retrace their way, and compelling them to follow each other, the narrowness of the passage preventing them from coming alongside of each other, or even wearing so as to bring their broadsides to bear. The commander of the Julia opened fire with his long 32, and in a short time the Simcoe, which was in advance, was disabled, and her consorts were as rapidly as possible trying to retrace their course. Although completely at his mercy, the gallant commander of the Julia did not deem it prudent to attempt to take possession of the Simcoe, because of her greater superiority in men, and, besides, there was always the chance that some of the enemy's vessels might gain his rear; so, deeming discretion the better part of valor, he gave the Simcoe a parting shot or two, and made his escape up the river, joining the fleet on Lake Ontario. For this gallant action Mr. Trant was promoted to a lieutenancy.

Many years ago, where the Pullman House now stands, Mr. Grinnell kept one of the old time "taverns," the like of which is seldom found in these days, and from time to time many distinguished personages became his guests for the sake of the hunting and fishing, not even excepting royalty itself, in the person of Count Surveiliers, alias Joseph Bonaparte, ex-king of Naples and of Spain. Those granite rocks up yonder, o'ertopped with a row of beautiful cottages, are named Jersey Heights. You should land here some day and take a look at "Grinnell" Island, and also at the new Park on the head of Murray Island.

Our next stopping place is at the Thousand Island Park landing, in full view of the stately Columbia hotel, and of many of the

MANNING & DAVIS,

DEALERS IN FINE

WINES, LIQUORS AND CIGARS.

All Leading Brands of Imported and Domestic Ales, Lagers and Mineral Waters.

MILWAUKEE, ROCHESTER AND ST. LOUIS LAGERS ON TAP.

We make a specialty of furnishing Cottagers and Camping Parties with first class goods at fair prices.

NEAR STEAMBOAT LANDING.

ALEXANDRIA BAY, N. Y.

Always the very
BEST
That can be had. At prices consistent with
QUALITY.

The Thousand Island Meat Market,

SAM B. MILLER, Proprietor,

ALEXANDRIA BAY, N. Y.

Caters to the Best Island Trade.

THE COLUMBIA HOTEL AT THOUSAND ISLAND PARK.

THE BIJOU PAVILION

THOUSAND ISLAND HOUSE,

ALEXANDRIA BAY, N. Y.

HEADQUARTERS FOR SOUVENIRS OF THE THOUSAND ISLES.

Huyler's Candies received daily from New York.

Japanese Goods.

White-Wood Souvenirs, View Books and Photographs.

Indian Baskets, Canoes and Curiousities.

Reading Matter of all Kinds. All the Latest Novels.

AGENT FOR MAJOR HADDOCK'S GREAT "SOUVENIR OF THE ST. LAWRENCE RIVER."

E. W. ESTES

elegant cottages of this beautiful summer city of the St. Lawrence. Here are all the modern conveniences, electrical lights, water works, telegraph and telephone communication, a steamer for some point almost every hour in the day, excellent bathing, splendid fishing, and, in fact, an ideal summer home. I need not enter into a detailed description here, as you will find its history printed in full elsewhere. Directly in front of the landing are the "Lone Tree" and "Twin" Islands. We next touch at the wharf in front of the "Fine View House"—one of the many pleasant hotels on the river—and only ten minutes walk to the Thousand Island Park. On the right is the pleasant little hamlet of Fisher's landing, "Occident" and "Orient" islands, and, a little below them, Fredericks' Islands, owned by a merchant of Carthage, N. Y.

Along the shore of Wellesley Island, on our left, is a long line of delightful cottages, among which is "Hiawatha," the quaint cottage of Prof. Hoose, an eminent educator, and the group of cottages, "The Jolly Oaks," among which are those of Mr. J. L. Norton, a prominent merchant of Carthage, and Hon. W. W. Butterfield, of Redwood, N. Y. The next place of any special importance is "Peel Dock," and thereby hangs a tale; " and here it is.*

Burning of the Steamer "Sir Robert Peel."

Those who have kept themselves informed on matters of history will remember that, on the 29th day of December, 1837, the steamer Caroline, an American steamboat, while lying tied to the wharf at Schlosser, a port on the Canadian side of the Niagara river below Buffalo, was boarded by a band of Canadians, robbed, set fire to, cut loose from her moorings, and sent burning over Niagara Falls. This caused great indignation throughout the country, and added much to the excitement consequent on the breaking out of the so-called Patriot war, which was, in fact, a weak rebellion on the part of some dissatisfied Canadians, with which a number of United States citizens very foolishly took sides. The steamer Sir Robert Peel was new and staunch, built at Brockville only the year before, and owned by both Canadian and American citizens. She was sailed by Capt. John B. Armstrong. Starting from Prescott on the afternoon of the

---

*Bear in mind, however, that until the occurrence here related took place, this was called " McDonnell's Wharf," and not " Peel Dock,"

Summer ∴ Resort.

THE NEW
HAY ISLAND
HOUSE.

In the midst of the far-famed Thousand Islands
Of the renowned River St. Lawrence.

GANANOQUE P. O.
ONTARIO, CANADA.

J. DE WITTA, Proprietor.

This Commodious Summer Resort has recently been enlarged and refitted throughout in first-class style. The House is situated ¾ of a mile from, and commands a full view of, the old and picturesque Town of Gananoque, (pop. 4,000) which may be reached by train or boat. The Royal Mail Line steamers, the New Island Wanderer (on her daily trips) and all other vessels pass closely to and in full view of the House, between which and the Town the main channel passes.

The Island contains about 125 acres, there being a beautiful yard and grove adjoining the House. The Main Building is 84 x 30, the sleeping apartments 13 x 10—newly plastered—some with connecting doors. The Dining Rooms in a separate building.

The Island is situated in the very midst of the famous 1000 Island group—over 60 of the same being in full view. The best fishing grounds in the River surround the Island. Oarsmen, boats and fishing outfits at reasonable rates. Splendid bathing facilities—safe for children.

Terms for board and lodging, $6 per week and upwards, according to rooms.

For further particulars apply to the proprietor.

29th of May, 1838, she touched at Brockville on her way to Toronto, having on board a cargo and nineteen passengers. She arrived at McDonnell's wharf at midnight to take on wood. It had been hinted to the captain before leaving Brockville that there was danger ahead, but he disregarded the warning. The passengers were asleep in the cabin, and the crew had almost finished their labor of taking on wood, when a party of twenty-two men, disguised and painted like Indians, and armed with muskets and bayonets, rushed on board, yelling like savages, and shouting, "Remember the Caroline!" They drove the passengers and crew ashore, allowing but little time for the removal of baggage belonging to them, the most of which was lost. The steamer was fired in several places, and the party left in two boats, steering for Abel's Island, about four miles away, which they reached at sunrise. The ill-fated steamer sunk in mid-channel but a short distance below the wharf where she was captured, and there she now lies twenty fathoms deep, while we sail to and fro directly over her wreck.

The leader of this party was William Johnston, better known to fame, or notoriety rather, as "Bill Johnston," a Canadian outlaw, around whose career, and that of his daughter Kate, the once famous novelist, "Ned Buntline" (E. Z. C. Judson), threw a halo of mystery and romance. Bill Johnston was born at Three Rivers, Lower Canada, February 1, 1782. His parents removed to, or near, Kingston, in 1784, and at the breaking out of the war of 1812, he was a grocer in Kingston, and a member of a military company. For an act of insubordination, it is said, though what was its nature is not now apparent, he was tried by a court martial, lodged in jail, and his property confiscated. Escaping thence he came to the States, and became the bitterest and most vindictive foe Canada ever had. He acted as a spy for the Americans during the war of 1812-15, robbed the British mails, and committed every depredation possible upon Canada and Canadians. After the burning of the Sir Robert Peel, he was outlawed by both the United States and Canadian governments, who tried in every way possible to effect his capture; but his hiding places were so numerous, and so many were his personal friends, that, with the aid of his daughter Kate, who kept him supplied with food, which she took to him in the dead of night in her skiff alone, and with news of his enemies, also, that they succeeded in capturing him but twice, both of which times he escaped ;

ECHO LODGE,
THOUSAND ISLANDS.

This new Summer Resort is situated in the very heart of the Thousand Islands, in a beautiful, secluded and picturesque spot near the celebrated "Fiddler's Elbow," in view of the "Lost Channel" and within speaking distance of the famous "Echo Rock." Fishing and Scenery are acknowledged to be the grandest on the River St. Lawrence.

Conveyance meets all trains at Lansdowne Station, G. T. R. ; only a few minutes drive and easily accessible by boat from Alexandria Bay, Rockport, Kingston and Gananoque.

Those requiring rest, seclusion, and home comforts will do well to write for particulars to

O. L. POTTER, Proprietor,
IVY LEA P. O., ONTARIO.

REASONABLE RATES BY THE WEEK.

Steamer "Princess Louise," from Kingston, calls at Echo Lodge every Friday and Saturday, leaving Kingston at 4.00 P. M.

R., W. & O. R. R. DOCKS, AT CLAYTON, N. Y.

The "Corsican" is the Canadian boat, plying between Kingston and Montreal. At this wharf all the regular Folger boats stop, up and down, as well as upon the Rambles we are trying to describe.

Thousand Islands,   St. Lawrence River.

JEFFERSON HOUSE, Alexandria Bay, N. Y.

Z. Bigness, Proprietor.   R. H. Service, Clerk.

Enlarged and Refurnished throughout. First-class Bar with Restaurant attached. Everything New. Good Barn Accommodations. Rates, $2.00 per day, 50 cents a meal.

though if the stories told of his hair-breadth escapes, whether true or not, were written down, they would fill a book. Finally, when matters became quiet, he returned to his home in Clayton, and in time was appointed keeper of the Rock Island light, whose rays illumine the very spot over which once shone the light of the burning steamer Sir Robert Peel.

On our left, as we leave Peel Dock, is a lovely little white cottage on "Island Kate," the residence of the late Mrs. Tomlinson, of Watertown, N. Y. In a short time we swing out from the main channel and pass, on our left, the miniature "Island of St. Helena," with its batteries of Quaker guns. The surface of the island, curiously enough, is almost a *fac simile* of St. Helena itself; and so the genial owner, H. Stillman, Esq., of Oswego, has utilized the idea, and thus we have every prominent point located, even to the tomb of Napoleon. If there were only a miniature Napoleon on the island, with a miniature Sir Hudson Lowe for his jailer, the illusion would be complete. On our right is "St. Lawrence (formerly Central) Park." Here is a fine hotel, and a group of beautiful summer homes, owned by Rev. Richmond K. Fisk, Ayers, Mass.; C. W. Hackett, of Utica, N. Y.; Hon. Charles R. Skinner, of Albany, State Superintendent of Public Instruction; J. F. Moffet, Hon. B. B. Taggart, W. G. Williams, Judge P. C. Williams, and H. F. Inglehart, all of Watertown, N. Y.

We touch, for a moment, at "Point Vivian," a collection of beautiful cottages on the mainland, and then away for Alexandria Bay.

On our left is "Hill Crest" and "Shady Covert," the property of B. J. Maycock, of Buffalo. On our right we approach "Wild Rose Island," the property of Hon. W. G. Rose, of Cleveland, O., which is connected with "Gypsy," owned by J. M. Curtis of the same city, by a beautiful bridge of a single span, not a "bridge of sighs," but a bridge of joys. Opposite, Gen. Van Patten, of Claverack-on-the Hudson, has a fine location, and then comes "Seven Isles," the beautiful summer home of Gen. Bradley Winslow, of Watertown, N. Y.; "Louisiana Point," owned by the late Judge Labatte, of New Orleans, and the beautiful cottage, known as "Lambie Point," owned by the Messrs. Lambie, of Theresa, N. Y.

We now approach the lower channel group, leaving "Bell Vista," "Nehmabin," "Comfort" and "Greystone Villa" on our left, passing "Wauwinet," "Keewaydin" and "Cuba," and now the steamer,

HOTEL FRONTENAC.
KINGSTON, CANADA.

Opens on June 10th to October 1st for Summer Tourists.

Special rates for Parties during the Summer Months.

Rates, $2.50 to $3.50.

THOS. CRATE, Proprietor.

with a square turn to the left, runs so close to the "Devils Oven" that you can almost touch it, and then heads toward "Castle Rest."

On the left it may be that the visitor will again this season greet the "Red Cross," the summer home of one of the grandest women of the age, the Florence Nightingale of America, Miss Clara Barton, of Washington, D. C. To the soldier, wounded and dying, she was

DEVIL'S OVEN.

an angel of hope. To the earthquake and tornado-stricken people of the South, she was an angel of relief; and to the stricken, everywhere, whether by war, famine or pestilence, she was an angel of Mercy; she has won the applause of nations and the admiration of the world. In the midst of destitution, disease and death she has borne the sacred emblem to the relief of thousands, and no one has a better right than she to exclaim, "*In hoc signo vinces!*" Let us rejoice that she is an American woman, and, because of her grand

STEAMER SPRY.

THIS IS ONE OF THE FINEST BOATS ON THE ST. LAWRENCE RIVER. ELEGANTLY FURNISHED WITH ALL MODERN IMPROVEMENTS. WILL CARRY COMFORTABLY 24 PEOPLE. CAN BE CHARTERED BY THE DAY OR SEASON ON REASONABLE TERMS. HAVE FOR SALE THE

CELEBRATED ST. LAWRENCE RIVER SKIFFS,

OF MY OWN MAKE. I HAVE OVER 30 YEARS' EXPERIENCE IN BOAT-BUILDING. CALL AND SEE MY BOATS, IT IS NO TROUBLE TO SHOW THEM.

Capt. JOHN H. DINGMAN,
ALEXANDRIA BAY, N. Y.

efforts in the cause of humanity, accord to her, that which she has so nobly won, our highest admiration and respect.

Then comes the summer camp of Rev. Royal Pullman, and "Hopewell Hall," the property of W. C. Browning, of New York; "Castle Rest," the minature of Ehrenbreitstein, one of the old castles on the Rhine, and then, in succession, come: "Friendly," E. W. Dewey, New York; "Nobby," H. R. Heath, New York; "St. Elmo," N. W. Hunt, Brooklyn, N. Y.; "Welcome," S. G. Pope, Ogdensburg, N. Y.; "Felseneck," Prof. Hopkins, Hamilton College; "Linlithgow," Mrs.

NOBBY ISLAND.

Robert Livingston, New York; "Florence," H. S. Chandler, New York; "Isle Imperial," Mr. Rafferty, Pittsburg, Pa. These are among the Central, or Bay group, and now we swing to the wharf at Alexandria Bay, with its elegant hotels — the Metropolis of the Thousand Islands.

But we must on with our trip. As we swing out into the stream and head away on our course, we leave "Bonny Castle," the property of Mrs. J. G. Holland. This was the favorite summer home of that gifted author and editor, Dr. James G. Holland, whose name is a household word, and whose fame is world-wide, and whose death

STEAMER SPRY, CAPT. G. H. DINGMAN. [SEE PAGE 34.]

was a national loss, because he was one of our most gifted authors. To the world of letters his loss was irreparable. On our left is "Manhattan," thought by many to be the most beautiful island in the river, owned by Judge J. C. Spencer, of New York; "St. John's," Judge Chas. Donahue, of New York; "Fairyland," with its three beautiful villas, belonging to the Messrs. Hayden, of Columbus, O., and "Hugnenot," the summer home of L. Hasbrouck, of Ogdensburg, N. Y. Down the main channel, at our right, is "Resort Island," owned by W. J. Lewis, of Pittsburg, Pa., and along the mainland are: "Long Branch," owned by Mrs. Clark, of Watertown, N. Y.; "Point Marguerite," the summer home of the late Edward Anthony, of New York; "The Ledges," C. J. Hudson, New York.

The Tweed Ring.

Close on our right is "Deer Island," as it was once called, now "Pine Island," "Old Picnic Island" and "Lotus Land." Pine Island was at one time the summer resort of the famous "Tweed Ring," of New York, away back in 1870. That was when the now magnificent Crossmon House was only a plain country tavern, though always a good one. Mrs. Crossmon, the honored mother of the present genial proprietor, well remembers baking "Boston brown bread" for them, and many citizens of Alexandria Bay remember well the "high old jinks" held by the gang on their visits to the river. Who was the gang? Just glance at the list: The three first, William M. Tweed, Hank Smith and William R. Stewart, were the "bosses." They concocted the schemes, and the others carried them into effect. Here was Foster Dewey, Tweed's private secretary; Andrew J. Garvey. Cornelius Carson, Boss Tweed's confidential clerk; Peter B. Sweeney and Dick Cornell, and then there was a lot of sub-lieutenants besides. Up here, they styled themselves the "Medicus Club," and "bad medicine" they were too, though judging from the fact that they doctored New York city to the amount of $27,000,000, the name was very appropriate.

We now bear away to the right, leaving "Pine Island," "Old Picnic" and "Lotus Land" on our right, and enter the "Friendly" or "Boundary Group." This is one of the loveliest scenes on the whole river, and we sail through its very midst. Here are "Little Lehigh," "Sport," "Idlewild," "Summerland" and "Arcadia" islands, on

THE "NEW ISLAND WANDERER."

which are the beautiful cottages of Messrs. W. A., R. H. and E. P. Wilbur, all of Bethlehem, Pa.; Mrs. R. H. Eggleston, New York; S. A. Briggs, of New York, and a group of Rochester families. You will acknowledge that this view alone is worth taking the afternoon ramble to see, and it is only one of the Thousand Island Steamboat Company's boats, either the Islander or America, that can pass through this group.

On leaving it, we head away toward "Rockport," a little hamlet on the Canadian mainland, passing on our starboard, or right-hand side, the head of "Geenadier" Island, with its red-capped Canadian Light-house, "Little Grenadier," "Doctor" and "Star" islands. The latter was formerly called "Tar" Island, but the addition of a single letter has done wonders for it. Gen. Bradley Winslow, of Watertown, N. Y., has a fine farm on Star Island. His elegant cottage was burned in 1892. It is one of the most sightly and romantic spots on the river. At our left is Westminster Park, a beautiful resort at the foot of Wellesley Island, as the Thousand Island Park is at its head, and at the foot of "Hill" Island, the charming villa, with its tasteful surroundings, of D. F. Fairchild, of Leavenworth, Kansas, classically named Fairjoline. A ferry plies hourly between Westminster Park and Alexandria Bay, and from this point a narrow passage leads into Lake "Waterloo," its outlet in fact, a trip to which, as I have already advised, you should not fail to take.

On our right comes the little Canadian hamlet of Rockport, and on our left is "Club Island" on which are the beautiful summer homes of Mrs. F. Taylor, of New York, and Jacob A. Skinner, Esq., of Newark, N. J Then comes "Echo Point," of which we will get auricular demonstration, if the steam holds out. Just opposite us, and about midway of this palisade of granite rock, is an Indian painting, easily distinguishable from the deck of a smaller boat that can run close enough in. It represents a wild animal in the act of leaping upon a warrior, though it would require a label to tell us what species of animal was intended.

Through what scenes of nature's own loveliness we have just passed! They have been the theme of writers innumerable, and poets have exhausted the power of song in their praise. It was here that Tom Moore, in 1803, only a year previous to his death, was inspired by the goddess of song, which a few days later found vent in that magnificent poem :

POPULAR BAY AND HOTEL WESTMINSTER.

> "Faintly as tolls the evening chime,
>   Our voices kept tune, and our oars keep time;
>   Soon as the woods on shore look dim
>   We'll sing at St. Ann's our parting hymn.
>   Row, brothers, row; the stream runs fast,
>   The rapids are near, and the daylight is past.
>
> "Why should we yet our sail unfurl?
>   There is not a breath the blue wave to curl!
>   But when the wind blows off the shore,
>   Oh! Sweetly we'll rest on our weary oar.
>   Row, brothers, row; the stream runs fast,
>   The rapids are near, and the daylight's past.
>
> "Utawa's tide! This trembling moon
>   Shall see us float o'er thy surges soon.
>   Saint of this green isle! Hear our prayer,
>   Oh! grant us cool heavens and favoring air.
>   Blow, breezes, blow; the stream runs fast,
>   The rapids are near, and the daylight is past."

But the most beautiful tribute to the Thousand Islands ever written must be awarded to one of Canada's own poets, Joseph Octave Crémazié. His poem was published in "Histoire de la Litterature Canadienne," in 1850, and again in 1860, by M. Larean, Vol. II, page 107. I can only find room for a translation of two stanzas:

"When Eve plucked Death from the Tree of Life, and brought tears and sorrow upon the Earth, Adam was driven out into the world to mourn with her, and taste of the bitter spring that we drink from to-day.

"Then Angels on their wings bore the silent Eden to the Eternal Spheres on high, and placed it in the Heavens—but in passing through space, they dropped along the way, to mark their course, some flowers from the Garden Divine. These flowers of changing hue, falling into the Great River, became the Thousand Islands—the Paradise of the St. Lawrence."

Next comes the widely known "Lost Channel," and in justice to one of the best pilots on the St. Lawrence river, the man who above all others originated these "Island Rambles," Capt. Visgar, of Alexandria Bay, I must accord a generous meed of praise, because no man better deserves it.

Early comprehending the fact that this group of islands, situated comparatively near to Alexandria Bay, which was destined to become the metropolis of the Thousand Islands, would attract the attention of large numbers of visitors and tourists, he began to turn his attention to the means for gratifying their very laudable curiosity, and scored a grand success. And so, to Capt. Visgar alone belongs the honor of having explored the different channels, and led the way through the most intricate windings of these delightful archipelagoes of the noble St. Lawrence.

On one occasion, while passing through a difficult channel below and a little to the right of the Fiddler's Elbow as we go down the river, a correspondent of the New York *Tribune*, who was on board, called out: "Captain! what is the name of this channel?" Captain Visgar, busy at the wheel, and fully occupied in seeing that his boat passed safely through the difficult passage, and not caring to be disturbed at a critical moment, answered: "This, sir, is the Lost Channel." The reporter "took down" the answer, and in due time the *Tribune* had a lurid description of the Thousand Islands, and a thrilling account of the passage of the "Lost Channel."

Just there was where Captain Visgar "builded better than he knew;" for while the "Lost Channel" became an object of curiosity far and wide, and a trip through it something to be desired, not one visitor out of a thousand was aware of the fact that it had a history which went back a hundred and thirty-five years, and yet such is the case. I will give it as briefly as possible, referring you to Major Haddock's admirable Souvenir History of the Thousand Islands for a more elaborate account.

History of the Lost Channel.

During the French and English war, which began in 1755 and ended in 1760, an expedition was fitted out at Oswego, in August of the latter year, for the final subjugation of the Canadas. The only

remaining strongholds of the French were Montreal, and a strong
fort on an island in the St. Lawrence river, about three miles below
the present city of Ogdensburg, known as Fort Levis, commanded
by a distinguished French officer — Capt. Pouchot. The expedition
consisted of 10,142 British regulars and Colonial troops from Massachusetts, Connecticut, New York and New Jersey. Among the
Massachusetts troops was Israel Putnam, of Revolutionary fame,
then a lieutenant-colonel. In addition to these troops, there was a
force of about 1,000 Indians, under the command of Sir William
Johnson. The commander of the expedition was Gen. Jeffrey
Amherst, the second in command being Gen. Gage, of Boston fame.
At that time the English had two armed vessels on Lake Ontario,
the *Onondaga* and the *Mohawk*, commanded by Capt. John Loring,
as Admiral of the fleet, which consisted of the two vessels, 177
batteaux and 72 whale boats, besides staff boats, hospital boats, and
boats for sutler's use. The first detachment of troops sailed in the
two vessels, on the 7th of August, for the rendezvous at "Basin
Harbor," Grenadier Island, at the head of the St. Lawrence river.
On the 13th, the entire army were assembled on the island, and early
on the morning of the 14th the entire expedition set forth. Capt.
Loring, with the two vessels, had gone ahead, and instead of keeping
straight down the South channel, he crossed just below the foot of
Wolfe Island into the Canadian channel. The French had been
expecting an attack from this direction for a whole year; and, in
consequence, had kept a lookout on Carleton Island, from which
point they could readily see when the British forces entered the
river; and with swift war canoes they could easily convey the intelligence to the fort below. When Capt. Loring had fairly entered
the Navy group, he was assailed on every hand. The islands seemed
to swarm with French and Indians, who were raking his decks with
musketry. To add to his discomfiture, he knew nothing of the
river nor of the labyrinth of islands in which he found himself;
but, lowering away a boat and crew, he sent them back to prevent
the Mohawk from entering the island group; and manning his guns,
he swept the islands around him with grape and cannister, as he
drifted with the current, he knew not whither. Fortunately, he got
safely clear of the islands, when, coming to an anchor, he sent two
other boats to find the first one sent out, but they returned unsuc-
cessful; nor could they even distinguish which of the channels was
the one in which the first boat was lowered. They never saw boat

nor crew again; and ever afterward, in speaking of it, they called it the "Place of the Lost Channel." Two or three years later, the crew of a batteau found a broken yawl boat bearing the name "Onondaga," at the head of one of the channels, which, since that time, has been known as the "Lost Channel," and which Capt. Visgar so happily renamed. The probability is that the crew of the yawl boat were killed and scalped by the Indians, and their boat stove and sunk; and, after all, we have no absolute certainty that this, more than any other of the numerous channels on every hand, was the one in which Capt. Loring first lowered his yawl boat. All that Capt. Loring's journal says about that part of it is the simple statement that they "called it the place of the lost channel."

Next in order is the little island called "Fiddler's Elbow." Why this island was so named is accounted for in two ways. One is, that it used to be a great camping place for the crews of batteaux long before the day of steamers on the river, and that usually there was a fiddler among them who furnished music for their rude dances. The other is that a shrewd old river pilot who used to bring his passengers to view this group of islands, took care to have a venerable old fiddler, who lived in a shanty near by, always on hand and playing for dear life when the boat passed. Then, again, the shape of the island suggests the crook in a fiddler's elbow. You may suit yourself as to the hypotheses.

Swinging to the left we pass "Ash Island" on our right and reach "Lyndock Light." Away to our left is "Boundary Channel," which leads into "Lake Waterloo," or, as it is commonly known, the "Lake of the Island," a place you should not fail to visit. Passing these we head away through the Halstead Bay group; leaving "Anderson's Camp" on our right and "Smoke Island" on our left, we enter "Halstead's Bay," and direct our course for Gananoque.

The lower end of Halstead's Bay terminates in a long arm, which extends for some distance inland. Here are the "Indian Rocks" and "Horseblock Point." On a precipice which forms a part of the point, there was clearly visible only a few years ago some aboriginal paintings, representing a hunting scene, but by whom painted no one could tell; even the tribes which were here when the white man first came, knew nothing of their origin. To-day but little is to be seen of them, though under a favorable light it is said that the outlines are yet to be distinguished.

There is another way through this labyrinth of islands that is, if possible, more interesting than this. It takes us nearer to the Canadian shore, running close into "Ivy's Mills," past "Champagne Point" and through a beautiful net-work of little islands, bringing us out again at the head of the Lost Channel. The steamer "Islander" sometimes makes a special trip through those channels, and if the opportunity occurs, you should not fail to see that part of the group, for the "Islander" is a superior boat, well officered.

On our left now is "Stone Island," "McDonald's" and "Sugar" islands, and a beautiful group of small islands near the shore of Grindstone Island. But we push on to Jackstraw light and prepare to stop at Gananoque. This is a busy manufacturing village and will well repay a visit of some hours. I forgot to tell you that the large group of islands, through which we have just passed, is called the "Navy" group, and that the group through which we are about to pass is called the "Admiralty" group, and from the fact that the Canadian islands are known by numbers instead of names, it is not easy to designate them clearly; but so far as they have become private property, they are named, and those, to some extent, we will point out.

As we swing out from the wharf at Gananoque, Tidd's island, on which is a lovely summer resort, is at our left, and to our right is "Hog" island. At "Dorsdale," R. Forsyth, Esq., of Montreal, spends his vacation; Rev. Prof. Mowat, of Queen's College, Kingston, is at "Riverview," and Prof. Coleman, of Victoria College, Coburg, Ont., makes "Weidenfeldt" his summer home; Mr. Camp, of Toronto, owns "Idlewild," and then comes the cottages of C. E. Britton, Esq., and Dr. A. N. Kincaid, both prominent citizens of Gananoque. On our left, again, J. Findley, Esq., of Montreal, occupies "Round Island," and on the right is the cottage of Rev. J. Allen, of Coburg, Ont. Then comes "Sylvan Isle," J. L. Upham, Esq., of Brockville, Ont.

On our left the cottages, in succession, are: "Camp Iroquois," Mr. Wallace, of Boston; "Roseneath Villa," Jas. Richmond, Esq., of Kingston; "Channel View," Jno. Turcotte, Esq.; "The Castle," Prof. N. F. Dupuis, of Queens College; on our right, "Burnt Island" light, and on our left is "Boss Dick Island." The beautiful group, through which we have just past, is Bostwick channel, one of the finest among the island groups.

BONNY CASTLE.
Summer residence of the late Dr. J. G. Holland.

Station Island.

You have, no doubt, read that thrilling tale of Fenimore Cooper's, "The Pathfinder." If so, you will remember the episode of "Station Island," its description, how it was situated, and for what purpose it was garrisoned. Cooper, in "The Pathfinder," makes no attempt to locate the island. He only relates some historical facts connected with it, and gives us a minute description of it. The time described was during the French and English war of 1755-60. At that time the English held Oswego, while the French had control of the lakes with a strong fort at Frontenac, now Kingston, and a detachment at Gananoque. The French received their supplies from Montreal in batteaux which came up the river in detachments, numbering ten or more batteaux each. The English kept spies on the lookout for the arrival of these convoys of stores and provisions with a view to their capture. To that end "Station Island" had been fixed upon as a suitable place for a rendezvous from which to waylay the expected fleet of batteaux. It was to protect this fleet that a party of French and Indians had been stationed at Gananoque.

Now what are the historical facts? First, the French posts were supplied from Montreal by means of batteaux; second, the British troops attempted to, and did at various times, capture some of these batteaux with their stores; third, that the British had some hiding place among the islands, from which they sallied forth and made their captures, if possible. Now it is evident that this very group of islands would be the one chosen for such a hiding place for several reasons. First, it was nearer Oswego; second, the chances of recapture were lessened; third, the opportunity of watching the approach of a fleet of batteaux unseen. If the hiding place had been chosen in the Lower or Naval group, the chances of a recapture would have been materially increased. Now how was "Station Island" situated? So that a look-out could be kept on the river below; so that the French post on the main land could be watched; so that the island itself could hardly be distinguished from those by which it was surrounded. One island in this group fulfils the conditions, and there is not another among all the Thousand Islands that does; and hence the presumption that the island is here, and that it borders on Bostwick channel. To one who is fond of exploration it will be a half day's pleasure to search it out, and then if you fail to find it, ask the guide on the steamer. During the war of 1812, Gananoque was the scene of a daring assault on the part of a detachment of American troops from Sacket's Harbor, the particulars of which are as follows:

Expedition Against Gananoque.

On the night of the 20th of September, 1812, Gen. Brown dispatched Capt. Benjamin Forsyth with a force of ninety-five men, from Sacket's Harbor, with a view of capturing some ammunition, of which his troops stood greatly in need. Capt. Forsyth and his men landed at a point about two miles above the village, and at daylight began their march on the place. When about half way they were met by two horsemen, one of whom was shot, and the other escaped and gave the alarm. A force of 110 men at once opposed the advance of the Americans. Halting within a hundred yards of the English line of battle, Capt. Forsyth ordered his men to fire a volley, and charge. The order was obeyed, and the British were driven back with a loss of several killed and wounded and a dozen prisoners. The spoils were 3,000 ball cartridges, and forty-one muskets. Not having boats to take them away, 150 barrels of provisions were burned, as also was the King's Store. It was only the next year that the British had their revenge out of Capt. Forsyth, for they whipped him badly at Ogdensburg.

Swinging around toward the completion of our grand circle, we reach the group of islands at the head of Grindstone Island. On our right the largest of the group is "Hickory Island." It was on this island that the so-called "Patriots" made a stand in the winter of 1837. They had collected a strong force, and were amply provisioned, but without a leader, order or discipline,— simply a mob. On the approach of a small force from Kingston, with a piece of light artillery, they fled without firing a shot, leaving the most of their stores behind. It was a perfect stampede; and to use the language of an eye witness: "I wouldn't wonder if some of them were running yet."

On the left are "Coral" and "Club" islands, on the former of which is the beautiful Japanese Villa, owned by Mr. C. Wolfe. Other cottages are owned by Thomas Thatcher, Esq., of Boston; Mrs. Moore, Harry Morgan and Bryant Lindley, Esqs., all of New York.

We now head away for Clayton, passing through the Blanket shoals, and leaving Bartlet's Point on our right, and "Governor" and "Calumet" islands to our left, on the latter of which is the elegant palace-cottage belonging to Chas. G. Emory, Esq., of New York. Bartlet's Point is now called "Prospect Park." It was first named Bartlet's Point, because a man of that name settled there in 1801 and ran a ferry to Gananoque. It is said of him that he set his house on fire and ran away by the light of it. Away yonder to our right you see that a bridge spans the outlet of French creek, a con-

ONE OF THE FOLGER STEAMERS.

siderable stream that flows into the bay here; just above that bridge once stood an Iroquois fort, or rather a Huron fort, which was captured from them by one of the Iroquois tribes — the Oneidas. That must have been fully 200 years ago. The creek was called by the Indians *Weteringhea Guentere*. But there was quite a skirmish there in 1813, when the American troops under Gen. Brown, being the advance of that ill-fated expedition under Wilkinson, which was so badly whipped by the British at Chrysler's farm only a few weeks later, was attacked by a British force. The following is a brief history of the affair, which you can read at your leisure:

The Battle of French Creek.

Gen. Jacob Brown, commanding the advance of Gen. Wilkinson's expedition, arrived at French Creek on the evening of October 30, 1813, and on the next day crossed a part of his command to the opposite shore, and awaited an expected attack. By his direction, Capt. McPherson, of the U. S. Light Artillery, had erected a battery on Bartlet's Point and mounted three long eighteen pounders. From his elevated position, Capt. McPherson could command the entrance to the bay and pretty effectually shell the entire peninsula on which the village of Clayton now stands.

On the evening of November 1st, the attack was made by a fleet of two schooners, two brigs, and several boats loaded with troops. The first attempt was made upon Capt. McPherson's battery, but the guns were so well served, and so accurate was their fire, that the vessels were soon forced to drop down the river, beyond the range of the battery. The next morning the attack was renewed. The troops were landed on the peninsula, below where the village now stands, and marched across to the attack. In the meantime, Forsyth's riflemen had been deployed in the woods as skirmishers, and met the advancing troops with a galling fire, which threw them into confusion. Simultaneously with the landing of the troops, the vessels again attacked the battery on Bartlet's Point, but with less success than at first. Three of them were so disabled in a few minutes that they were glad to drift down the river and out of range; and the fourth, deeming discretion the better part of valor, withdrew. The troops, seeing their vessels disabled, made a precipitate retreat, and thus ended the battle of French Creek.

And now, dear Rambler, we have completed a circle of nearly if not quite sixty miles in circumference, and arrived at our starting point. The thing now to do is to round out the day by taking the Search Light ramble to-night, a description of which you will find in another place.

The Search Light.

For this trip we board the steamer St. Lawrence, for the reason that it has the most powerful Search Light on the river, and was the first to bring these fascinating trips into popular notice, and is besides the largest steamer on the river that gives these Search Light excursions on so grand a scale. There are other considerations, too, which you will note as you go along, not the least of which is the fact that the science of electricity has made these trips a nightly possibility, because of the element of absolute safety that it has brought into play. Before the Search Light came, a night trip among the river archipelagoes was an affair of moonlight. No pilot, however skillful, cared to thread the tortuous channels in a moonless night. Now, the situation is changed. A cool-headed captain and a careful mate and skillful wheelsman, with an expert electrician, as the steamer St. Lawrence always has, and barring accidents which no man can foresee, a trip among the islands on a night of inky blackness is as safe as an easy chair at home. Skill and science united have reduced danger to a mere nothing.

As before, we board the steamer at Alexandria Bay, and start up the river. First on one shore and then on the other, the Search Light sends a flood of radiance that illumines every spot it touches, as with the glare of a noonday sun; camp and cottage, leafy covert and rocky glen, all stand revealed. Here a flood of light reveals happy groups on porch and balcony of hotel and cottage, and there a leafy covert becomes a bower of brilliancy, while eerie shadows dark as Erebus flee away into inky depths. It is a succession of transformation scenes never equaled elsewhere.

Touching at all points on our way up the river, we stop for a short time at Clayton and then head away across the river for the passage between Grindstone Island on our left, and "Robbins'" Island on our right, known as "Robbins' Cut." All the way up the river we have been greeted with rockets and red fire, and even now they have not ceased. Passing "Calumet Island," on our left, we approach a jolly camp on Grindstone Island, where cheers and fireworks seem to spring forth spontaneously; and then on we go through the long narrow channel, lighted alternately from side to side, and out into the broad waters of "Eel Bay," passing "Point Angier," "Elephant Rock," "Picnic" and "Squaw" Points on our left, and then swinging off toward the lights in the "Grand View Park" Hotel. A place, by the way, well worth a visit. On our right as we speed along is a group of but little more than bare rocks, known as "Robinson's" or "Indian" Islands. Should we be signaled, we will stop a moment at Grand View Park, but if not we head away for "Lyndock" Light at the entrance to the "Navy" group and so down past the "Fiddler's Elbow," on through the group past Echo Point, past Rockport, and across through the Bay Group and home to Alexandria Bay, in good time for bed, or for the "hop" at the hotel; just as we feel inclined. Reader, our regular rambles are ended, and now with your kind permission I will suggest, without entering into any special description, a few

Other Trips.

I have already hinted that a trip to "Ivy's Mills," and among the beautiful islands bordering that part of the mainland, is a very desirable one. It is true that, as yet, no regular trip has been established through this part of the Navy Group, but the time is not far distant when the demands of sightseers will be complied with and new ramble routes opened, and, among them all, this divergence from the present route will be very popular because of its beauty.

The trip through "Boundary Channel," and to "Waterloo Lake," should not be forgotten, especially the latter. Until the steamboat companies provide for a regular trip to these places, you can always charter a small steam yacht, with a competent pilot, to explore them. The better plan is to make up a party; and in this way the cost of the trip is not great, and if a fine day be chosen, it cannot fail to be one of great pleasure.

Another pleasant side trip is to "Goose Bay," and the beautiful island group—"Dinkelspiel"—at its entrance. "Cranberry Creek," which was the scene of quite a sharp skirmish during the war of 1812, flows into Goose Bay. I give you a brief sketch of the affair, hoping that it may not be entirely devoid of interest.

Battle of Cranberry Creek.

This was one of the most stirring affairs that took place among the Thousand Islands during the war of 1812-14; and seems to be the only case on record where a deputy collector of a port exercised the authority to grant letters of marque; but such is the fact in this case, and whether there are other instances of a like nature remains to be seen.

Be that as it may, on the 14th of July, 1813, two armed boats, the Fox and Neptune, the latter a private craft, armed with one 6-pounder and a swivel, the former a government boat, left Sacket's Harbor under letters of marque, issued by the deputy collector of the district. The Neptune was manned by twenty-four volunteers, under the command of Capt. Samuel Dixon, and the Fox, commanded by Capt. Dimmock, by twenty-one men of the Twenty-first Infantry, under Lieutenants Burbank and Perry, and a detachment of the Forsyth Rifles, under Lieut. Hawkins and Sergt. James.

The expedition was fitted out by Marinus W. Gilbert, of Watertown, with the object of cutting off a detachment of the enemy's boats, which were expected to arrive up the river about this time, laden with stores. The two boats touched at Cape Vincent on their way down the river, and made a short halt at French Creek, now Clayton, and then pushed on to Cranberry Creek, where they held a review, put their boats in complete order, examined and cleaned their arms, and then sent forward an express to Ogdensburg for intelligence. At five o'clock in the afternoon of the second day the looked-for intelligence came, and at nine o'clock that night the two boats left the creek and pulled across the river into the Canadian channel, and at four o'clock in the morning they discovered a brigade of the enemy's batteaux lying at "Simmon's Landing," under the protection of His Majesty's gunboat Spitfire, just ready to proceed to Kingston.

Pushing rapidly to the shore, Lieutenant Perry with Sergeant James and twenty-seven men landed to cut off their retreat, while Captain Dixon, with Lieutenant Burbank and the remainder of the men took possession of the batteaux and gunboat. So complete was the surprise, that the fifteen batteaux and the gunboat with their crews, were captured without a single shot being fired on either side, and by nine o'clock in the morning they were safe in Cranberry Creek again, and Lieutenant Burbank started at once for Sacket's Harbor, with a detachment of fifteen men and sixty-nine prisoners.

In the meantime news had reached Kingston and a force was sent to recapture the gunboat and batteaux, consisting of four gunboats, and the Earl of Moira, an eighteen-gun brig; and on the morning of the 21st, just as the rising sun tipped with gold the island summits, the four gunboats manned with 250 men were discovered entering Goose Bay and making their way to the mouth of the creek.

Thirty men met them and gallantly disputed their landing, while twenty more took up a position from which they could successfully dispute their further advance; and in the meantime the six-pounder opened a rapid and galling fire which seriously disabled two of the British gunboats, the crews turning their attention to plugging the shot-holes in them. In a short time the enemy retired to the boats and after pulling beyond gunshot, sent in a flag of truce demanding a surrender to "stop the effusion of blood," which was answered by an advance of our men, and reopening the fire on the gunboats, when they hurriedly retreated, and the battle of Cranberry Creek was over. The casualties on our side were two men killed and one wounded, while the British loss is, by their own authorities admitted to have been twelve killed and several wounded, besides the loss of Captain Milnes, a gallant officer, and aid-de-camp to the "Commander of the Forces."

The capture was of great value, but owing to the fact that some of the batteaux were hurriedly sunk without orders, it proved to be an unprofitable expedition to its promoters. The lading of the batteaux consisted of 270 barrels of pork and 270 bags of hard bread, most of which were scattered and wasted in some way; at all events they failed to reach Sacket's Harbor, although the expedition returned safely, meeting its only mishap when rounding Tibbett's Point; it was fired upon by the Earl of Moira, and though some of the boats were struck by her shot, they all escaped.

There is another pleasant trip to be taken, which leads us down along the American shore and through a fine group of islands in "Chippewa Bay," the largest of which is "Oak" Island, formerly known as "Indian Hut" Island. As long ago as when Count Frontenac was the commander of the French forces in Canada, an Indian, familiarly known as the Quaker, because of his peaceful proclivities, obtained a grant from the count, of this island; and with a number of families of his tribe, made a considerable settlement upon it. He had been much among the French and was extremely fond of imitating their courtly manners, though his efforts to do so were, at times, extremely ludicrous. He affected all the airs and graces of Count Frontenac himself, and regarded the Indian settlers on his island in the light of subjects over whom he exercised a mild sovereignty.

His aboriginal lordship was too fond of the "fire-water," however, and so he sold his domain one day for a jug of rum, but he retained a life lease, and continued to play the sovereign until King Death preferred his claim and ended the lease. There are beautiful cottages on some of these islands, and more will be erected in the near future. The little hamlet of Chippewa Bay was visited by a British force from Canada during the war of 1812, but it retired without doing any great damage. This part of the Thousand Islands is well worth seeing, and though as yet none of the steamboat managers have made any special provision for visitors to travel this route, it is one that ere long the traveling public will demand to see, and then it will not be long before the means are provided.

From Chippewa Bay, we steam directly across the river, passing over the scene of a naval engagement in 1813, between the American schooner Julia, and the British schooner Earl, in which the Julia got the worst of it and fled to Ogdensburg. It was on the same spot, also, that the British, under General Amherst, in 1760, captured a French brig. On our way, we pass Cedar, Dark and Corn Islands, and a beautiful group named respectively, Pearl, Cherry, Narrow, Little, Suma, and Tent Islands. Close to the Canadian shore is Chimney Island, on which at one time there were fortifications; probably during the War of 1812. Turning up stream we pass inside of "Grenadier" Island, and find hidden away there another beautiful cluster of islands, the principal ones of which are Pooles, Senecals, and O'Neils. It is along this shore that a writer has laid the scene of an interesting tale, entitled the "Witch of Plum Hollow," founded on an old legend of the vicinity. Passing out into the main channel at the head of Grenadier Island, we steam away for Alexandria Bay, having had one of the most enjoyable trips on the river.

Fort Haldimand.

The ruins of this very elaborate fortification are situated on a bluff at the head of Carleton Island, about eleven miles above Clayton, and in the middle of the American Channel. This fort was erected by the British. It was begun in 1778, the next year after the surrender of Burgoyne at Saratoga. For some years, it was the most important military and naval station on the St. Lawrence river, or on the lakes even, above Montreal. There are some of the old barrack chimnies yet standing, and the earth-works are very distinct, while the ditch, which was cut in the limestone rock, is the same as ever. The outer parapet and glacis have been much damaged by the removal of the stone of which they were built. The places of the garrison well, the magazines, the bastions and salients are distinct and easily located. This island played an important part in the war of the Revolution. Here was the home of the noted Thayendanegea, alias Joseph Brandt, the chief of the Six Nations. It was from this island that the expeditions against Wyoming, Cherry Valley, and Fort Edward, bloody massacres all, were sent out. The fort was built after the plans of Lieut. Twiss, Burgoyne's chief engineer, who afterward became Lieutenant-General Twiss, the greatest military engineer Great Britain ever had; and by him the fortification was named Fort Haldimand, in honor of Gen. Sir Frederick Haldimand, under whose orders the fort was built, and who at that time was commander-in-chief of His Majesty's forces in Canada. At the same time, the name of the island was changed from "Deer" Island to "Carleton" Island, in honor of Sir Guy Carleton, afterward Lord Dorchester. Under the cliff on which the ruins of the old fort are situated is a beautiful peninsula with a lovely bay on either hand. During the British occupation this was called "Government Point;" and was given up to the use exclusively of the naval officers and artificers. There was a large shipyard on the Point, and many vessels of war and gunboats were built there.

Now, the "Government Point" of those days is occupied by the grounds of the Utica Club and several private cottages, one of which, Capt. Wyckoff's, of the firm of Wyckoff, Seamans & Benedict, of New York, is one of the finest and costliest on the river. It is up here, too, where the best black-bass fishing in the world is to be had.

Kingston.

Of course you will not fail to board that most magnificent of river steamers the "Empire State," for a visit to Kingston, the Fort Frontenac of the French. There are many places of interest in Kingston well worth a visit. To an American, unacquainted with Canadian cities, Kingston has a series of surprises in store, and a day or two may be profitably spent there. Fort Henry, the Military College, the Artillery Barracks, on the site of Old Fort Frontenac, the Cathedral, the Dominion Penitentiary, the Insane Asylum, and a round trip on the Electric Railway — which last enables you to see the most in the least time — are among the interesting points to be visited, and if your stay is limited, take the Electric Railway trip by all means; because it describes a complete circle through all the best portions of the city

Special Trips.

Several times, during the season, one or another of the elegant steamers of the Thousand Island Steamboat Company, will make a special excursion to Morrisburg, a quaint but pleasant Canadian

THE DITCH AT FORT HALDIMAND.

town, about twenty miles below Ogdensburg. During this trip the steamer runs the "Galloup Rapid" and the "Rapide du Plat." Below Ogdensburg, and on the opposite side of the river, is the Old Windmill, made famous during the so-called Patriot war of '37, though why called "Patriot" does not appear so clearly, and still lower down is "Chimney Island," on which are the remains of Fort Levis, the last stronghold of the French on the St. Lawrence, and taken by Gen. Jeffrey Lord Amherst in 1760. You will find this a very interesting excursion and one you cannot afford to miss.

"Picton," and the "Lake on the Mountain."

This is another special trip afforded by the Thousand Island Steamboat Company several times during the season. Not only does the tourist, on this trip, experience the pleasure of viewing the delightfully romantic scenery of the "Bay of Quinte," and a visit to one of its pleasantest villages, but he will have the pleasure of inspecting one of the greatest natural phenomena known to this or any other country. The "Lake on the Mountain" has attracted the attention of scientists from every part of the civilized world. It is a huge spring, widening out to the dimensions of a pond, situated upon the summit of a ridge which lies between Lake Ontario and "Bay de Quinte," and more than a hundred feet above either. I have not the exact figures within reach, but my impression is that the "Lake" is over 150 feet higher than the level of Lake Ontario. Be that as it may, it furnishes a constant supply of water sufficient to propel a large amount of machinery, and never fails. It is really worth a visit for itself alone, without the other pleasant features of the trip as an accompaniment.

I might suggest other special trips to you, but they would take me beyond the original scope of this booklet. In describing to you the trips among the Islands, it is very probable that I have made some errors, either of omission or commission; and if it be so, it is really not to be wondered at, because I have written almost entirely from memory. Then, too, new places are springing up; new cottages are in process of erection every summer, and new names are adopted; so that what may be correct this season, may be wrong the next. However, what is wrong in this edition will be gladly set right in the next, for we expect to keep pace with the times and seasons.

L'Envoi.

And now, dear Rambler, we have spent some pleasant hours in our excursions together, and I hope we may spend many more; and when toward life's close we look back to the many enjoyments experienced among the beautiful scenery of the Thousand Islands, let us hope that not a single regret will cast its shadow across the bright retrospect. To me, these rambles are always pleasant, and if I have added a mite to the sum total of your enjoyment, I am content. Au revoir!

Island Directory.

The following is a late revised list of islands and points, with their owners' names, from Clayton to Goose Bay, on the American side:

Cement Point, head of Grindstone Island, owned by W. F. Ford and others.

Goose Island, two acres, owned by E. S. Brooks, Brooklyn.

Hen Island, one-half acre, owned by W. F. Morgan, New York.

Davitts' Island, one-quarter acre, owned by H. G. Davitts, New York.

Carroll Island, two acres, owned by Jas. A. Cheney, Syracuse.

Boscobel Island, one-half acre, owned by G. S. Hopkins, Kansas.

Bluff Island, twenty acres, owned by E. B. Washburn, New York.

Clinton Island, No. 1, fifteen acres, owned by N. S. Seely, New York.

Clinton Island, No. 2, three acres, owned by N. S. Seely, New York.

Governor's Island, owned by Chas. G. Emery, New York.

Calumet, owned by Chas. G. Emery, New York.

Etheridge, head of Round Island, owned by Dr. Geo. D. Whalen, Syracuse.

Shady Ledge, foot of Round Island, owned by Frank R. Taylor, Philadelphia, Pa.

Brooklyn Heights, foot of Round Island, owned by C. S. Johnson, Brooklyn.

Long Rock, one acre, owned by W. F. Wilson, Watertown.

Hemlock Island, twenty acres, owned by W. F. Porter and W. F. Wilson, Watertown.

Stewart, or Jeffers, Island, ten acres, owned by E. P. Gardiner and twelve others, Syracuse, and other places.

Two in Eel Bay, two acres, owned by Dr. E. L. Sargent, Watertown.

Twin Islands, one acre, owned by J. L. Huntington, Theresa.

Watch Island, one acre, owned by S. F. Skinner, New York.

Occident and Orient, three acres, owned by E. N. Robinson, New York.

Isle of Pines, two acres, owned by Mrs. E. N. Robinson, New York.

Frederick Island, two acres, owned by C. L. Frederick, Carthage.

Bay Side, one acre, owned by H. F. Mosher, Watertown.

Riverside, mainland, one acre, owned by J. C. Lee, Gouverneur.

Killain Point, mainland, one acre, owned by Mr. Killian, Lockport, N. Y.

Holloway Point, mainland, one acre, owned by N. Holloway, Omar, N. Y.

Fisher's Landing, mainland, two acres, owned by Mrs. R. Gunn, Omar, N. Y.

Island Home, one acre, owned by Mrs. S. D. Hungerford, Adams, N. Y.

Harmony, one-quarter acre, owned by Mrs. Burger, Syracuse.

Waving Branches, on Wells' Island, owned by D. C. Graham and nine others.

Bonnie Eyrie, on Wells' Island, owned by Mrs. Peck, Boonville, N. Y.

Throop's Dock, on Wells' Island, owned by Drs. C. E. and D. S. J. Latimer, New York.

Jolly Oaks, on Wells' Island, twenty acres, owned by Prof. A. H. Brown and four others.

Blanch Island, ten acres, owned by Mrs. A. M. Kenyon, Watertown.

Josephine, twenty acres, owned by Mrs. A. M. Kenyon, Watertown.

Craig Side, Wells' Island, owned by H. A. Laughlin, Pittsburg, Pa.

Covert Point, Wells' Island, owned by B. J. Maycock, Buffalo.

Calumet Island, one-half acre, owned by Oliver H. Green, Boston.

Van Patten, one acre, owned by Gen. J. B. Van Patten, Claverack, N. Y.

Point Vivian, mainland, ten acres, owned by R. Toyer and ten others.

Lindress, one acre, owned by John Lindress, Jersey City.

Isle Royal, one acre, owned by R. E. Deane, New York.

Cedar Island, one acre, owned by J. M. Curtis, Cleveland, O.

Wild Rose, one acre, owned by Hon. W. G. Rose, Cleveland, O.

Alleghany Point, mainland, one acre, owned by J. S. Laney, Pa.

Plato, two acres, owned by H. R. Heath, Brooklyn.

Seven Isles, five acres, owned by Gen. Bradley Winslow, Watertown.

Louisiana Point, Well's Island, three acres, owned by Hon. D. C. Labatt, New Orleans.

Bella Vista Lodge, mainland, five acres, Wm. Chisholm, Cleveland, O.

Neh Mahbin Island, two acres, owned by James H. Oliphant, Brooklyn.

Comfort Island, two acres, owned by A. E. Clark, Chicago.
Warner's Island, one acre, owned by Mrs. H. H. Warner, Rochester.
Wanwinet Island, one-half acre, owned by C. E. Hill, Chicago.
Kewaydin, owned by J. W. Jackson, Plainfield, N. J.
Cuba, one acre, owned by M. Chauncey, Brooklyn.
Devil's Oven, one acre, owned by H. R. Heath, Brooklyn.
Sunnyside, Cherry Island, five acres, Rev. George Rockwell, Tarrytown.
Melrose Lodge, Cherry Island, owned by A. B. Pullman estate, Chicago.
Ingleside, Cherry Island, owned by Mrs. G. B. Marsh, Chicago.
Stuyvesant Lodge, Cherry Island, owned by J. T. Easton, Brooklyn.
Safe Point, Wells' Island, four acres, Rev. R. H. Pullman, Baltimore.
Pullman Island, three acres, owned by Geo. M. Pullman, Chicago.
Nobby Island, three acres, owned by H. R. Heath, Brooklyn.
Little Angel, one-quarter acre, owned by W. A. Angell, Chicago.
Edgewood Park, thirty acres, owned by S. W. Sessions, Cleveland, O.
Edgewood Point, one acre, owned by G. C. Martin, Watertown.
West View, one acre, owned by S. G. Pope, Ogdensburg.
Welcome, one acre, owned by S. G. Pope, Ogdensburg.
Friendly Island, three acres, owned by E. W. Dewey, New York.
Linlithgow, one-half acre, owned by Mrs. R. A. Livingston, New York.
Florence, two acres, owned by H. S. Chandler, New York.
St. Elmo, three acres, owned by N. W. Hunt, Brooklyn.
Felseneck, owned by Prof. A. G. Hopkins, Clinton, N. Y.
Point Lookout, one acre, owned by Miss S. J. Bullock, Adams.
Vilula Point, one-half acre, owned by Capt. F. Dana.
Isle Imperial, one acre, owned by G. T. Rafferty, Pittsburg.
Fern Island, one acre, owned by J. Winslow, Watertown.
Hart's Island, five acres, owned by E. K. Hart's estate, Albion, N. Y.
Deshler, fifteen acres, owned by W. G. Deshler, Columbus, O.
Netts, one acre, owned by Wm. B. Hayden, Columbus, O.
Bonny Castle, fifteen acres, owned by Mrs. J. G. Holland, New York.
Crescent Cottage, ten acres, owned by B. Van Wagoner, New York.

62   THE RAMBLER.

Point Marguerite, thirty acres, owned by Mrs. E. Anthony, New York.

The Ledges, owned by Mrs. C. J. Hudson, New York.

Long Branch, ten acres, owned by Mrs. C. E. Clark, Watertown.

Manhattan Island, five acres, owned by Hon. J. C. Spencer, New York.

Maple Island, six acres, owned by John L. Hasbrouck, New York.

St. John Island, six acres, owned by Hon. Charles O'Donohue, New York.

Fairyland Island, twenty acres, owned by Charles and William B. Hayden, Columbus, O.

Little Fraud Island, one-half acre, owned by R. H. Pease, New York.

Huguenot Island, two acres, owned by L. Hasbrouck, Ogdensburg.

Resort Island, three acres, owned by W. J. Lewis, Pittsburg.

Deer Island, twenty acres, owned by Geo. D. Miller, New York.

Island Mary, two acres, owned by Geo. A. Lance, Watertown.

Walton Island, seven acres, owned by N. J. Robinson, New York.

Idlewild, four acres, owned by Mrs. R. A. Packer, Sayre, Pa.

Sport Island, four acres, owned by E. P. Wilbur, Mauch Chunk, Pa.

Little Lehigh, one acre, owned by R. H. Wilbur, Bethlehem, Pa.

Summer Side, two acres, owned by W. Stevenson, Sayre, Pa.

Summerland, ten acres, owned by Summerland Association, Rochester.

Arcadia and Ina Islands, five acres, owned by S. A. Briggs, New York.

Spuyten Duyvel, one acre, owned by Alice P. Sargent, New York.

Douglass, five acres, owned by Douglas Miller, New York.

Kit Grafton, one-half acre, owned by Mrs. S. L. George, Watertown.

Lookout, two acres, owned by Thos. H. Bordin, New York.

Ella, one-half acre, owned by R. E. Hungerford, Watertown.

Little Charm, one-quarter acre, owned by Mrs. F. W. Barker, Alexandria Bay.

Frost, two acres, owned by Mrs. S. L. Frost, Watertown.

Excelsior Group, five acres, owned by C. S. Goodwin, New York.

Sylvan and Moss Islands, three acres, owned by S. T. Woolworth, Watertown.

Elephant Rock, one-quarter acre, owned by T. C. Chittenden, Watertown.

THE RAMBLER.   63

Sunbeam Group, one acre, owned by A. B. Phelan.
Alice, two acres, owned by Col. A. J. Casse, New York.
Schooner, six acres, owned by J. N. Whitehouse, New York.

List of Post-offices Among the Thousand Islands, during the Season.

Thurso; Grindstone Island.
Clayton.
Round Island (summer only).
Grinnell's (summer only).
Thousand Island Park.
Fisher's Landing.
St. Lawrence Park (summer only).
Point Vivian (summer only).
Westminster Park (summer only).
Alexandria Bay.
Grand View Park (summer only).

Table of distances from Alexandria Bay.

To Montreal	148 miles	To Riverview	20 miles
To Ogdensburg	36 "	To Carleton Island	23 "
To Morristown	24 "	To Cape Vincent	28 "
To Brockville	24 "	To Gananoque	19 "
To Chippewa Bay	12 "	To Kingston	34 "
To Point Vivian	2 "	To New York	356 "
To St. Lawrence Park	3 "	To Boston	339 "
To Fine View	6 "	To Philadelphia	447 "
To T. I. Park	7 "	To Saratoga	239 "
To Fishers' Landing	7 "	To Chicago	812 "
To Pullman House	7½ "	To Niagara Falls	298 "
To Grand View Park	12 "	To Toronto	185 "
To Round Island	10 "	To Syracuse	122 "
To Clayton	12 "	To Utica	119 "
To Prospect Park	12 "	To Rochester	213 "

A few "Don'ts" for Excursionists.

Don't be in too great a hurry, you will get along easier.

Don't rush to get on board the steamer until the passengers are off, and then you can get on board without rushing.

Don't push, and jam, and crowd, either in going ashore or aboard; you only hinder and delay.

Don't stop to gossip on the gang-plank, it blocks the passage and delays others.

Don't act as though you thought that other people had no rights which you were bound to respect.

Don't act as though you belong to the genus *Sus*, lest people believe it.

Don't crowd to the forward part of the boat; the after part passes the same objects of interest.

Don't stand up, so that those back of you can see nothing — it is extremely ill mannered.

Don't try to gather in all the easy chairs just for your party — it looks selfish.

Don't be continually grumbling, you annoy others and do yourself no good.

Don't be too critical about the running of the boat; in all probability, those who have charge of it are as well informed in regard to their business as you are.

Don't berate an employé, because of some fault you think the company has committed — it is inconsistent.

Don't fail to treat others with that consideration with which you would like to have them treat you, and then all will go well.

You have often heard it said that such a one "could be a gentleman, if he chose;" you may rest assured that if any one *can be* a gentleman (or lady) he or she is pretty certain *to be* one; so, when on an excursion don't be anything else, lest people thinking that you *can be* but *will not;* attribute your actions to pure and unadulterated "cussedness," and treat you accordingly.

Canada's West Point.

With a frontier extending across a continent, bordering on a nation from which several hostile raids on behalf of "Irish Independence" have taken place, and with a halfbreed and Indian population in her own north-west, which has on two occasions broken out into open rebellion, Canada finds it necessary to maintain the nucleus of a military force, which shall be available on short notice to defend her frontier or to put down rebellion. She cannot afford to maintain a standing army, but she has three batteries of artillery on permanent service, and a cavalry school, four infantry schools, and one mounted-infantry school, at which the officers and non-commissioned officers of the Volunteer Militia may receive such a training as will fit them to take command and give instruction to the volunteers, who, taken from the field or workshop, would otherwise be wholly untrained and undisciplined.

But while her volunteers have given a good account of themselves when occasion called them into active service, and while her schools of military instruction have been the means of placing good officers at their head, it was felt that something more was needed to complete the system, and accordingly the Parliament of Canada, in 1874, passed an act authorizing the establishment of a Royal Military College "for the purpose," as the act states, "of imparting a complete education in all branches of military tactics, fortification, engineering and general scientific knowledge in subjects connected with and necessary to a thorough knowledge of the military profession, and for qualifying officers for command and for staff appointments."

In selecting a site for the college the government naturally turned its eyes to three places which were specially adapted for the purpose by virtue of their historical associations and the possession of extensive fortifications which might be utilized for technical training. These were Halifax, Quebec and Kingston. The latter was ultimately chosen, for, in addition to being the most central, it possessed certain buildings which could be utilized.

After the conquest of Canada, Kingston, the site of Fort Frontenac, built in 1673 by the French commander, after whom it was named, became a military post of great importance. During the war of 1812 it was the British naval station for the lakes. A dockyard was established on a low promonitory which juts out between the Cataraqui river and a small inlet of the St. Lawrence called Navy Bay. At this dockyard Sir James Yeo built his fleet for Lake Ontario. After the war the dockyard was dismantled, but a large three-story stone building remained, known as the Stone Frigate, which had been occupied by the marines. This, with a large blacksmith shop close by, was utilized for the college. [See buildings at left center of picture.]

In 1876 the first classes were opened, eighteen cadets being admitted. The staff consisted of a commandant, a captain and three professors. As the classes grew, more accommodation was required, and a large building, of the grey limestone for which Kingston is famous, was added. It contains offices, reading and mess-rooms, library, class-rooms, laboratory, hospital, and kitchen. The Stone Frigate became a dormitory, and the blacksmith shop was converted into a well-equipped gymnasium.

The main building faces a spacious parade ground, with tennis lawn and cricket ground, and opposite, on the point, is Fort Frederick, a battery which guards the entrance to the harbor, with a martello tower at its apex.

Though modeled after Woolwich, the college is intended to give the cadets a training which will fit them for civil as well as military life. The course, which is four years, though provision is made for a two years' course in certain subjects, embraces English, French, drawing, mathematics and mechanics, engineering, surveying, fortification, architecture, astronomy, chemistry, geology, mineralogy, physics, electricity, tactics and strategy, signaling, military law and administration, military drill, gymnastics, fencing, swimming and riding. A few of these subjects are voluntary, but most of them are obligatory. A rigorous examination has to be passed by candidates for entrance, and if more reach the minimum than can be admitted — two from each of the twelve military districts into which Canada is divided — those who make the highest number of marks are given the preference. The age of admission is from fifteen to nineteen.

The military staff consists of a commandant, staff adjutant and seven professors and instructors, four of whom are graduates of the college, and two of the latter hold commissions in the regular army. Five of the staff are officers of the active list of the imperial army, lent to the college for a five years' term, at the close of which they are required to rejoin their command. Two are officers of the retired list. There is a civil staff of five, holding permanent appointments from the government. The presence of imperial officers gives a standing to the institution which it would not otherwise possess, and helps the proper training of those of the cadets who are destined for commissions in the regular army. The government was fortunate in the choice of the first commandant, Col. Hewitt of the Royal Engineers, who, in addition to being an accomplished scholar and a good soldier, was possessed of great tact and energy, and knew Canada from former service. To his skill is due, in large measure, the success which attended the college from its very outset, and his guiding hand directed it through the difficulties which invariably attend the early career of a new institution, which, in this case, was to a large extent an experiment. Having completed his term he returned in 1886 to Plymouth, and was succeeded by Col. Oliver of the Royal Artillery, who had been professor of surveying and astronomy from the beginning, and who proved himself to be a worthy successor. The present head of the institution is Maj.-Gen. Cameron, late of the Royal Artillery.

Sir Frederick Middleton, now retired from the command of the Canadian forces, took a deep interest, officially and personally, in the college, and during its early days helped it with counsel and advice, which his experience at Sandhurst well qualified him to give. The general officer commanding the militia is *ex-officio* president of the college.

The entrance examinations are held in June at the headquarters of each military district, and the twenty-four successful candidates report themselves at the opening of the term the following September. The first week is spent in being uniformed and drilled into some kind of form. The second week the old cadets return, and the garrison settles down to hard work. The daily routine embraces drill and class parades, study and other duties. From reveille to tattoo, with the exception of two hours — from four to six, during which he is free — the cadet is under the eye of authority in the class or lecture-room or on parade. There is none of that loitering which so often takes place at civil colleges, none of that individual liberty which often means license. The cadet has, however, two half holidays, on Wednesday and Saturday, when he may go out on pass till eleven o'clock, or, with extra leave, till one. Balls and parties in Kingston are timed for these days, for the cadet, with his gay scarlet uniform, is an important factor in the social world. While attending the college the cadets are, of course, subject to the Queen's Regulations, the Army Act, the Militia Act, and such other rules and regulations as Her Majesty's troops are subject to.

The physical training is excellent. Sergt.-Major Morgan of the Scots' Guards presides over this department, and well qualified he is to fill the position. Cadets who pass four years under his instruction come out with deep chests and erect figures, and show what a thorough physical training can accomplish.

One of the rewards of good conduct is promotion to the rank of non-commissioned officer, the commandant having authority to appoint such from among those best qualified. Proud is he who is invested with the chevrons, or given the right to wear the sergeant's sash.

But while subject to strict discipline the cadets have opportunities to cultivate their social qualities. One of the events of the season is the annual sports, which take place in September. The campus is alive with carriages and pedestrians, while pretty girls, with their chaperons, form the center of groups engaged in animated conversation, or watching with interest the various competitions of speed and skill. Races, jumping competitions and steeplechases follow each other in quick succession, while the tug of war between the right and left wings creates almost as much interest as the struggle on the Isis between the college eights. The games over, all adjourn to the gymnasium, where the prizes, more substantial than the crown of ivy at the Olympic games, are distributed to the victors. Tea and an impromptu dance follow in the college halls.

A ball is given at Christmas by the staff and cadets, and a yet more elaborate entertainment of similar character at the close of the college year in June. On closing day a series of field manœuvers takes place, with blowing up of imaginary fortifications and fleets, and an exhibition of drill and bayonet exercise, after which the results of the examinations are announced, the prizes distributed, and the session brought to a termination. The governor-general, the minister of militia, or some one else high in authority, is secured, if possible, to distribute the prizes and make a speech. Four commissions, one each in the engineers, artillery, cavalry, and infantry branches of the imperial service, are available, the cadets who stand highest on the honor roll, if otherwise eligible, being entitled to them in the order named. The first two are eagerly sought, the third generally goes a-begging, as there are few Canadian youths with sufficient means to keep up a position in such an expensive branch of the service, in which case an additional commission in the infantry is generally substituted. All who have taken the full four years' course, and qualified in all the obligatory subjects, are entitled to receive a diploma of graduation, those who have specially distinguished themselves also receiving honors. Those who leave at the end of two years, and pass the subjects required, receive a certificate of military qualification only.

After the official proceedings are over on the closing day the cadets have a parade of their own, when the members of the graduating class have to undergo an ordeal of handshaking and leavetaking in true college form. A valedictory dinner in the evening follows, and then steamer and car bear the cadets off, and the halls are deserted for three months.

Some of the passed cadets of the college have already won fame for themselves. The name of Stairs, who accompanied Stanley in his march through darkest Africa, is well known the world over. Lieut. Hewitt served in the Soudan and bears a medal won on the banks of the Nile, and Lieut. Dobell has distinguished himself for bravery in Burmah.

Occasion has not yet arisen to call into full play the energies of the rapidly-growing members of the graduates of the Royal Military College, and it is, therefore, too early to judge of its full benefit to Canada. But the opinion of Lord Landsdowne, expressed when governor general, is worth quoting. These are his words:

"There is no Canadian institution of which Canada should be prouder or which will do better service to the country and to the empire. It forms an interesting and distinctive feature in the military system of the Dominion. That system, as I understand it, is based upon the recognition of the fact that Canada cannot afford in her own interests, or in those of the empire, to disregard those precautions which every civilized community takes in order to ensure its own safety from internal commotion or external attack. Upon the other hand, it is a system entirely opposed to the establishment of a numerous standing army, or to the withdrawal of a large body of citizens from the peaceful pursuits which are essential to the progress and development of the country.

"That being so, it is clear that, in case of a national emergency, the Dominion would have to trust largely to the spontaneous efforts of its own people, to the expansion of its existing organization, and the rapid development of the resources already at our command.

"But, gentlemen, it is needless for me to point out to you that there is one thing which it is impossible to produce on the spur of the moment, and that is a body of trained officers, competent to take charge of new levies or to supervise operations necessary for the defense of the national territory, and, therefore, it appears to me that we cannot overrate the value of an institution which year by year is turning out men who have received within its walls a soldier's education in the best sense of the word and who, whatever their primary destination, will, I do not doubt, be found available whenever their services are required by the country."

The cost of education at the Military College is not unreasonable. Each cadet is required to deposit annually $200 to cover the cost of messing and quarters, and in addition $200 the first year, and $150 each year afterwards for uniform, books and instruments. The messman receives forty-six cents per day for each cadet present. Extras are obtainable at fixed prices. No cadet is allowed to spend more than two dollars per month, non-commissioned officers more than four dollars, for extras, which they pay out of their pocket money.

In addition to the full course of four years and the military course of two years, provision has been made at the college for officers of the militia, who require higher instruction than the military schools afford, to take a three months' course, one class being instructed each year. By this means a number of officers have been enabled to qualify for important positions in the service.

Taken all in all, Canada's West Point has been an unqualified success.

"America."

The new steamer "America" has just been launched by the St. Lawrence River Steamboat Company. She is one of the most luxurious of the fleet under the management of that corporation. Their trio of "Empire State," "St. Lawrence" and "America," not to mention the other smaller boats, are unsurpassed by any steamers of their type in the world. The "America" is the same size as the "St. Lawrence," her frame-work and hull being of steel to correspond with that steamer. She has been planned in such a way that every demand of an exacting public will be gratified. Upon her main deck, aft, is located a large dining-room, equipped with individual tables, comfortable chairs, and the finest linen, crockery and glass-ware. This room is a model of taste and completeness; the heavy English brussels carpet, a delicate shade of olive green and gold, harmonizes with the rich velour curtains and wilton upholstery. Heavy, polished plate-glass windows extend from stem to stern on all decks, and every panel is filled with a beveled plate-glass mirror.

The range, tea and coffee urns, carving table and other culinary attributes have been specially manufactured to order by one of the best known makers on the continent. A visit to this department alone is extremely interesting and instructive, and will account for the excellent meals for which the Folger line is famous.

A large saloon cabin is built upon the promenade deck, and furnished in the same manner as the dining room upon the main deck, below. The staterooms, with which this steamer is well supplied, connect with the saloon cabin, and are equipped in a style consistent with the other tasteful and substantial furnishings.

The electric lighting is upon a most gorgeous scale, there being 250 incandescent lamps, whose radiant beauty is enhanced by artistic oxidized fixtures.

The search light is an exact duplicate in size, construction and power of the far-famed lamp of the Steamer "St. Lawrence." It is the largest ever seen on a passenger steamer, and in fact the extreme full size possible for such a purpose.

Owing to the stanchness of this beautiful boat, passengers have access to the hurricane deck, a privilege which everyone familiar with steamboats will appreciate. The interior decorative wood-work, arches, etc., in cabins is all carefully selected red oak, with stairs to match; the carving being executed by Wainright.

Among other unique features, introduced for the first time on this steamer, is one that deserves special mention : her wheels are of the most improved pattern of feathering bucket, so, instead of having them entirely concealed, and the beauty of their mechanism wasted, thick plate glass is inserted, through which one may observe the revolutions. Incandescent electric lights of various colors, with powerful reflectors are placed within the paddle boxes, and at night the irridescent rays illuminate the flying spray and produce a most weird and fascinating scene.

This new steamer is certainly a creditable addition to the "WHITE SQUADRON," which plys among the Thousand Islands in direct connection with the Vanderbilt system.

APPROACHING CLAYTON (THOUSAND ISLANDS).

Mr. John A. Haddock's Great Balloon Voyage With Professor LaMountain.

When the writer was in school at the Sulphur Springs in Houndsfield, under Professor Morsman, there were two kinds of English Readers then published by the firm of Knowlton & Rice, one containing Jaius Rich's story of his fight with the panther on Bluff Rock, below Theresa, the other edition failing to contain that narrative. The book with the panther story was eagerly sought and devoured by all the children who could read, while the other edition was not by any means regarded with affection. The intense impression made by that panther story upon my own mind and upon that of the other scholars, has been a matter of recollection through the sixty years which have elapsed. For that reason the author of this History has yielded to urgent solicitation, and presents below the story of his great aerial voyage in 1859 with John LaMountain, one of the longest voyages ever made in a balloon. The writer appears to be best remembered by that perilous episode, especially among those who are now the business men of Jefferson county, but who were then eager, pushing lads, nearly crazy over the balloon fever, which was at that time violent in Northern New York. Perhaps the most important result attained by that dismal balloon experience may be found in the article following this account, which relates to the "Awakening of Henry Backus."

The interest aroused by this balloon trip was surprising and almost phenomenal, my account being published at length in nearly every English newspaper. Perhaps the story illustrates fortitude under trying circumstances and under the agonizing strain experienced in the uncertainty which surrounded LaMountain and myself when toiling in that wildernes. In that light it may be regarded as an object lesson, not altogether to be lost upon those who are to come after us.

THE ACCOUNT.

It is now about thirty-five years since the undersigned made the memorable balloon voyage with Professor LaMountain—a voyage intended to be short and pleasant, but which resulted in a long and most disastrous one, entailing the loss of the valuable balloon, and seriously endangering the lives of the travellers. Since then, La-

Mountain, after serving through the great rebellion, has made his last "voyage," and has entered upon that existence where all the secrets of the skies are as well defined and understood as are the course of rivers here on earth.

To fully understand my reasons for making the trip, some leading facts should be presented:

1. There had been, all through the year 1859, much excitement in the public mind upon the subject of ballooning. In August of that year I returned from Labrador, and found that the balloon Atlantic, with Wise, Hyde, Gaeger and LaMountain, had been driven across a part of Lake Ontario, while on their great trip from St Louis to New York city, and had landed and been wrecked in Jefferson county, N. Y., and the people of that whole section were consequently in a state of considerable excitement upon the subject of navigating the air.*

2. I had heard of other newspaper editors making trips in balloons; had read their glowing accounts, and it seemed to me like a very cunning thing. Desiring to enjoy "all that was a-going," I naturally wanted a balloon ride too, and therefore concluded to go, expecting to be absent from home not more than ten or twelve hours at the longest, and to have a good time. Being a newspaper man, and always on the alert for news, I had also a natural desire to do all in my power to add to the local interest of my journal, and for

---

*The Wise named above was the celebrated aeronaut, Professor John Wise, of Lancaster, Pa.; and I may here remark that the trip made by him and his associates is by far the longest on record. Leaving St. Louis at about 4 P. M. they passed the whole night in the air, were carried across the States of Illinois, Indiana, a portion of Ohio and Michigan, over the whole northwestern breadth of Pennsylvania and New York, and were at last wrecked in a huge tree-top near the shore of Lake Ontario, at about 3 P. M. the next day, escaping with severe bruises but without broken bones, after a journey of eleven hundred miles. These adventurers did not travel as fast, nor encounter the perils that awaited us, but they made a longer voyage. It was with this same balloon Atlantic that LaMountain and myself made our trip, but it had been reduced one third in size, and was as good as new. John Wise afterwards lost his life in a balloon, but just where he perished was never known. Gaeger was a manufacturer of crockery, and he died in Massachusetts. Hyde is publishing a newspaper in one of the western States. LaMountain died in his bed at Lansingburgh, N. Y., about 1884.

that reason felt a willingness to go through with more fatigue and hazard than men are expected to endure in ordinary business pursuits.

3. I felt safe in going, as I knew that LaMountain was an intrepid and successful aeronaut, and I thought his judgment was to be depended upon. How he was misled as to distance, and how little he knew, or any man can know, of air navigation, the narrative will readily demonstrate.

With these explanations, I will proceed with my original narrative, nearly as written out at the time.

Nearly every one in Watertown is aware that the second ascension of the baloon Atlantic was advertised for the 20th of September, 1859. The storm of that and the following day obliged the postponement of the ascension until the 22d. Every arrangement had been made for a successful inflation, and at twenty-seven minutes before 6 P. M. the glad words, "all aboard," were heard from LaMountain, and that distinguished aeronaut and myself stepped into the car. Many were the friendly hands we shook—many a fervent "God bless you," and "happy voyage," were uttered — and many hankerchiefs waved their mute adieus. "Let go all," and away we soared; in an instant all minor sounds of earth had ceased, and we were lifted into a silent sphere, whose shores were without an echo, their silence equaled only by that of the grave. No feeling of trepidation was experienced; an extraordinary elation took possession of us, and fear was as far removed as though we had been sitting in our own rooms at home.

Two or three things struck me as peculiar in looking down from an altitude of half a mile: the small appearance of our village from such a height and the beautiful mechanical look which the straight fences and oblong square fields of the farmers present. As we rose into the light, fleecy clouds, they looked between us and the earth like patches of snow we see lying upon the landscape in spring-time; but when we rose a little higher the clouds completely shut out the earth, and the cold, white masses below us had precisely the same look that a mountainous snow-covered country does, as you look down upon it from a higher mountain. Those who have crossed the Alps — or have stood upon one of the lofty summits of the Sierra Nevada, and gazed down upon the eternal snows below and around them, will be able to catch the idea. In six minutes we were far above all the clouds, and the sun and we were face to face. We saw the time after that when his face would have been very welcome to us. In eight minutes after leaving the earth, the thermometer showed a fall of 24 degrees. It stood at 84 when we left. The balloon rotated a good deal, proving that were ascending with great rapidity. At 5:48 thermometer stood at 42, and falling very fast. At 5:50 we were at least two miles high — thermometer 34.

An unpleasant ringing sensation had now become painful, and I filled both ears with cotton. At 5:52 we put on our gloves and shawls — thermometer 32. The wet sandbags now became stiff with cold — they were frozen. Ascending very rapidly. At 5:54 thermometer 28, and falling. Here we caught our last sight of the earth by daylight, I recognized the St. Lawrence to the south-west of us, which showed we were drifting nearly north. At 6 o'clock we thought we were descending a little, and LaMountain directed me to throw out about 20 pounds of ballast. This shot us up again — thermometer 26, and falling very slowly. At 6:05 thermometer 22 — my feet were very cold. The Atlantic was now full, and presented a most splendid sight. The gas began to discharge itself at the mouth, and its abominable smell, as it came down upon us, made me sick. A moment's vomiting helped my case materially. LaMountain was suffering a good deal with cold. I passed my thick shawl around his shoulders, and put the blanket over our knees and feet. At 6:10 thermometer 18. We drifted along until the sun left us, and in a short time thereafter the balloon began to descend. We must have been, before we began to descend from this height, 3¼ miles high. At 6 : 22 thermometer 23 ; rising. We were now about stationary, and thought we were sailing north of east. We could, we thought, distinguish water below us, but were unable to recognize it. At 6 : 38 we threw over a bag of sand, making 80 pounds of ballast discharged, and leaving about 120 pounds on hand. We distintly heard a dog bark. Thermometer 28 — and rising rapidly. At 6 : 45 the thermometer stood at 33.

At 6 : 50 it was dark, and I could make no more memoranda. I put up my note book, pencil and watch, and settled down in the basket, feeling quiet contented. From this point until next morning I give my experiences from memory only. The figures given were made at the times indicated, and the thermometric variations can be depended on as quite accurate.

We heard, soon after dark, a locomotive whistle, and occasionally could hear wagons rumbling over the ground or a bridge, while the farmers' dogs kept up a continual baying, as if conscious there was something unusual in the sky. We sailed along, contented and chatty, until about half-past eight o'clock, when we distinctly saw lights below us, and heard the roaring of a mighty water-fall. We descended into a valley near a very high mountain, but as the place appeared rather forbidding, we concluded to go up again. Over with 30 pounds of ballast, and sky-ward we sailed. In about 20 minutes we again descended, but this time no friendly light greeted us. We seemed to be over a dense wilderness, and the balloon was settling down into a small lake. We had our life-preservers ready for use, but got up again by throwing out all our ballast, except perhaps 20 pounds. LaMountain now declared it was folly to stay up any longer, that we were over a great wilderness, and the sooner we descended the better. We concluded to settle down by the side of some tall tree, tie up, and wait until morning. In a moment we were near the earth, and as we gently descended I grasped the extreme top of a high spruce, which stopped the balloon's momentum, and we were soon lashed to the tree by our large drag-rope.

We rolled ourselves up in our blankets, patiently waiting for the morning. The cold rain spouted down upon us in rivulets from the great balloon that lazily rolled from side to side over our heads, and we were soon drenched and uncomfortable as men could be. After a night passed in great apprehension and unrest, we were right glad to see the first faint rays of coming light. Cold and rainy the morning at last broke, the typical precursor of other dismal mornings to be spent in that uninhabited wilderness. We waited until 6 o'clock in hopes the rain would cease, and that the rays of the sun, by warming and thereby expanding the gas in the balloon, would give us ascending power sufficient to get up again, for the purpose of obtaining a view of the country into which we had descended. The rain did not cease, and we concluded to throw over all we had in the balloon, except a coat for each, the life-preservers, the anchor and the compass. Overboard, then, they went — good shawls and blankets, bottles of ale and a flask of cordial, ropes and traps of all kinds. The Atlantic, relieved of this wet load, rose majestically with us, and we were able to behold the country below. It was an unbroken wilderness of lakes and spruce

—and I began to fully realize that we had indeed gone too far, through a miscalculation of the velocity of the balloon. As the current was still driving us towards the north, we dare not stay up, as we were drifting still farther and farther into trouble. LaMountain seized the valve-cord and discharged gas, and we descended in safety to the solid earth. Making the Atlantic fast by her anchor, we considered what was to be done.

We had not a mouthful to eat, no protection at night from the wet ground, were distant we knew not how far from any habitation, were hungry to start with, had no possible expectation of making a fire, and no definite or satifactory idea as to where we were. We had not even a respectable pocket knife, nor a pin to make a fish hook of—indeed we were about as well equipped for forest life as were the babes in the woods.

After a protracted discussion, in 'which all our ingenuity was brought to bear upon the question of our whereabouts, we settled in our minds (mainly from the character of the timber around us), that we were either in John Brown's tract, or in that wilderness lying between Ottawa City and Prescott, Canada. If this were so, then we knew that a course south by east would take us out if we had strength enough to travel the distance.

TRAMPING IN THE WOODS.

Acting upon our conclusion, we started through the woods toward the south-east. After traveling about a mile we came to the bank of a small stream flowing from the west, and were agreeably surprised to find that some human being had been there before us, for we found the stumps of several small trees and the head of a half-barrel, which contained pork. I eagerly examined the inspection stamp; it read :

"MESS PORK,"
"P. M."
"MONTREAL."

This settled the question that we were in Canada, as I well knew that no Montreal inspection of pork ever found its way into the State of New York. Although the course we had adopted was to be a south-easterly one, we yet concluded to follow this creek to the westward, and all day Friday we travelled up its banks — crossing it about noon on a floating log, and striking on the southern shore a "blazed" path, which led to a deserted lumber road, and it in turn bring us to a log shanty on the opposite bank. We had hoped this lumber road would lead out into a clearing or a settlement, but a careful examination satisfied us that the road ended here, its objective point evidently being the shanty on the other bank. We concluded to cross the creek to the shanty, and stay there all night. Collecting some small timbers for a raft, LaMountain crossed over safely, shoving the raft back to me. But my weight was greater than my companion's, and the frail structure sank under me, precipitating me into the water. I went in all over, but swam out, though it took all my strength to do so. On reaching the bank I found myself so chilled as scarcely to be able to stand. I took off all my clothes and wrung them as dry as I could. We then proceeded to the shanty, where we found some refuse straw, but it was dry, and under a pile of it we crawled — pulling it over our heads and faces, in the hope that our breath might aid in warming our chilled bodies. I think the most revengeful, stony heart would have pitied our condition then. I will not attempt to describe our thoughts as we lay there; home, children, wife, parents, friends, with their sad and anxious faces, rose up reproachfully before us as we tried to sleep. But the weary hours of night at last wore away, and at daylight we held a new council. It was evident, we argued, that the creek we were upon was used by the lumbermen for "driving" their logs in the spring freshets. If, then, we followed it to its confluence with the Ottawa or some stream which emptied into the Ottawa, we would eventually get out the same way the timber went out. The roof of the shanty was covered with the halves of hollow logs, scooped out in a manner familiar to all woodsmen. These were dry and light, and would make us an excellent raft. Why not, then, take four of these, tie them to cross-pieces by wythes and such odd things as we could find around the shanty, and pole the craft down stream to that civilization which even a saw-log appeared able to reach. Such, then, was the plan adopted, although it involved the retracing of all the steps hitherto taken, and an apparent departure from the course we had concluded would lead us out.

Without delay, then, we dragged the hollow logs down to the creek, and LaMountain proceeded to tie them together, as he was more of a sailor than myself. We at last got under way, and as we pushed off, a miserable crow set up a dismal cawing — an inauspicious sign We poled down the stream about a mile, when we came abruptly upon a large pine tree which had fallen across the current; completely blocking the passage of the raft. No other course was left us but to untie the raft, and push the pieces through under the log. This was at last accomplished, when we tied our craft together again, and poled down the stream. To-day each of us ate a raw frog (all we could find), and began to realize that we were hungry. Yet there was no complaining — our talk was of the hopeful future, and of the home and civilization we yet expected to reach. Down the creek we went, into a lake some four miles long, and into which we of course supposed the stream to pass, with its outlet at the lower end. We followed down the northern bank, keeping always near the shore and in shallow water, so that our poles could touch the bottom, until we reached the lower extremity of the lake, where we found no outlet, and so turned back upon the southern shore in quest of one. On reaching the head of the lake, and examining the stream attentively, we found that the current of the creek turned abruptly to the right, which was the reason of our losing it. We felt happy to have found our current again, and plied our poles like heroes. We passed, late in the afternoon, the spot where we had at first struck the creek, and where we stuck up some dead branches as a landmark which might aid us in case we should at a future time attempt to save the Atlantic.

When night came on we did not stop, but kept the raft going down through the shades of awful forests, whose solemn stillness seemed to hide from us the unrevealed mystery of our darkening future. During the morning the rain had ceased, but about 10 o'clock at night it commenced again. We stopped the "vessel" and crawled in under some "tag" alders on the bank, where our extreme weariness enabled us to get perhaps half an hour's sleep. Rising again (for it was easier to pole the raft at night in the rain down an unknown stream amidst the shadows of that awful forest, than to lie on the ground and freeze), we pressed on until perhaps three in the morning, when pure exhaustion compelled us to stop again. This time we found a spot where the clayey bank lacked a little of coming down to the water. On the mud we threw our little bundle of straw, and sat down with our feet drawn up under us, so as to present as little surface to the rain as possible.

But we could not stand such an uncomfortable position long, and as the daylight of the Sabbath broke upon us, we were poling down the stream in a drizzling rain. At 8 o'clock we reached a spot at which the stream narrowed, rushing over large boulders, and between rocky shores. This was trouble indeed. To get our raft down this place we regarded as well-nigh hopeless. We tied up and examined the shore. Here, again, we found unmistakable marks left by the lumbermen, they having evidently camped at this point, to be handy by in the labor of getting the timber over this bad spot in the stream. The rapids were about a third of a mile long, and very turbulent. After a protracted survey we descended the bank, and thought it best to abandon our raft, and try our luck on foot again. After travelling about a mile, we found the bank so tangled and rugged, and ourselves so much exhausted, that satisfactory progress was impossible. So we concluded to go back, and if we could get the raft down, even one piece at a time, we would go on with her — if not, we would build as good a place as possible to shield us from the cold and wet, and there await with fortitude that death from starvation which was beginning to be regarded as a probability. This was our third day of earnest labor and distressing fatigue, and in all that time we had not ate an ounce of food, nor had dry clothing upon us.

Acting upon our resolution we at once commenced to get the raft down the rapids, and I freely confess that this was the most trying and laborious work of a whole life of labor. The pieces would not float over a rod at a time, before they would stick on some stone which the low water left above the surface; and then you must pry the stick over in some way, and pass it along to the next obstruction. We were obliged to get into the stream, often up to the middle, with slippery boulders beneath our feet. Several times I fell headlong — completely using up our compass, which now frantically pointed in any direction its addled head took a fancy to. The water had unglued the case, and it was ruined. After long hours of such labor we got the raft down and LaMountain again tied it together. Passing on, in about an hour we came to a large lake, about ten miles long by six broad. Around it we must of course pass, until we should find the desired outlet. So we turned up to the right, and pressed on with as much resolution as we could muster. To-day we found one clam, which I insisted LaMountain should eat, as he was much weaker than myself, and had eaten nothing on the day we went up.

Part of this day LaMountain slept upon the raft, and I was "boss and all hands." As the poor fellow lay there, completely used up, I saw that he could not be of much more assistance in getting out. Erysipelas, from which he had previously suffered, had attacked his right eye; his face was shriveled so that he looked like an old man, and his clothes were nearly torn from his body. A few tears could not be restrained, and my prayer was for speedy deliverance or speedy death. While my companion was asleep, and I busily poling the raft along, I was forced to the conclusion, after deliberately canvassing all the chances, that we were pretty sure to perish there miserably at last. But I could not cease my efforts while I had strength, and so around the lake we went, into all the indentations of the shore, keeping always in the shallow water. The day at last wore away, and we stopped at night at a place we thought least exposed to the wind. We dragged the end of our raft out of the water and laid down upon the cold ground. We were cold when we laid down, and both of us trembled by the hour, like men suffering from a severe attack of the ague. The wind had risen just at night, and the dismal surging of the waves upon the shore formed, I thought, a fitting lullaby to our disturbed and dismal slumbers.

By this time our clothes were nearly torn off. My pantaloons were split up both legs, and the waistbands nearly gone. My boots were mere wrecks, and our mighty wrestlings in the rapids had torn the skin from ankles and hands. LaMountain's hat had disappeared; the first day out he had thrown away his wollen drawers and stockings, as they dragged him down by the weight of water they absorbed. And so we could sleep but little; it really seemed as though during this night we passed through the horrors of death. But at daylight we got up by degrees, first on one knee and then on the other, so stiff and weak that we could hardly stand. Again upon the silent, monotonous lake we went—following around its shore for an outlet. About 10 o'clock we come to quite a broad northern stream, which we thought was the outlet we were seeking, and we entered it with joy, believing it would take us to our long sought Ottawa. Shortly after entering this stream it widened out and began to appear like a mere lake. We poled up the western shore for about seven miles, but found ourselves again deceived as to the outlet —

the water we were upon proving to be another lake or bayou. We had gone into this lake with the highest hopes, but when we found that all the weary miles of our morning travel had been in vain, and had to be retraced, my resolution failed me for a moment. Yet we felt that our duty, as Christian men, was to press forward as long as we could stand, and leave the issue with a higher Power.

It had now been four full days since we ate a meal. All we had eaten in the meantime was a frog apiece, four clams and a few wild berries, whose acid properties and bitter taste had probably done us more harm than good. Our strength was beginning to fail very fast, and our systems were evidently undergoing an extraordinary change. I did not permit myself to think of food — the thought of a well-filled table would have been too much. My mind continually dwelt upon poor Strain's sufferings on the Isthmus of Darien (then lately published in Harper's Magazine). He, too, was paddling a raft down an unknown stream, half starved, and filled with dreadful forebodings. But I did not believe we could hold out half as long as he had. Besides, he was lost in a tropical country, where all nature is kind to man; he had fire-arms and other weapons with which to kill game. We were in a cold, inhospitable land, without arms and utterly unable to build a fire. Strain was upon a stream which he knew would eventually bear him to the sea and to safety; while we were upon waters whose flow we positively knew nothing about, and were as much lost as though in the mountains of the moon. Yet we could not give it up so, and tried to summon up fresh courage as troubles appeared to thicken around us. So we turned the raft around and poled it in silence back toward the place where we had entered this last lake. We had gone about a mile when we heard the sound of a gun, quickly followed by a second report. No sound was ever so sweet as that. We halloed as loud as we could a good many times, but could get no response. We kept our poles going quite lively, and had gone about half a mile when I called LaMountain's attention to what I thought was smoke curling up among the trees by the side of a hill. My own eyesight had begun to fail very much, and I felt afraid to trust my dulled senses in a matter so vitally important. LaMountain scrutinized the shore very closely, and said he thought it was smoke, and that he believed there was also a birch canoe on the shore below. In a few moments the blue smoke rolled unmistakably above the tree tops, and we felt that

WE WERE SAVED!

Such a revulsion of feeling was almost too much. We could hardly credit our good fortune, for our many bitter disappointments had taught us not to be very sanguine. With the ends of our poles we paddled the raft across the arm of the lake, here perhaps three-quarters of a mile wide, steering for the canoe. It proved to be a large one, evidently an Indian's. Leaving LaMountain to guard and retain the canoe, in case the Indian proved timid and desired to escape from us, I pressed hurriedly up the bank, following the footprints I saw in the damp soil, and soon came upon the temporary shanty of a lumbering wood, from the rude chimney of which a broad volume of smoke was rising. I halloed — a noise was heard inside, and a noble-looking Indian came to the door. I eagerly asked him if he could speak French, as I grasped his outstretched hand. "Yes," he replied, "and English, too!" He drew me into the cabin, and there I saw the leader of the party, a noble-hearted Scotchman named Angus Cameron. I immediately told my story; that we had come in there with a balloon, were lost, and had been over four days without food — eagerly demanding to know where we were. Imagine my surprise when he said we were one hundred and eighty miles due north of Ottawa, near 300 miles from Watertown, to reach which would require more than 500 miles of travel, following the streams and roads. We were in a wilderness as large as three States like New York, extending from Lake Superior on the west, to the St. Lawrence on the east, and from Ottawa on the south, to the Arctic circle.

The party consisted of four persons — Cameron and his assistant, and a half-breed Indian (LaMab McDougal) and his son. Their savory dinner was ready. I immediately dispatched the young Indian for LaMountain, who soon came in, the absolute picture of wretchedness. All that the cabin contained was freely offered us, and we began to eat. Language is inadequate to express our feelings. Within one little hour the clouds had lifted from our sombre future, and we felt ourselves to be men once more — no longer houseless wanderers amid primeval forests, driven by chance from side to side, but inspired by the near certainty of seeing home again and mingling with our fellows once more in the busy scenes of life.

We soon learned from Cameron that the stream we had traversed with our raft was called Filliman's creek — the large lake we were then near was called the Bos-ke-tong, and drains into the Bos-ke-tong river, which in turn drains into the Gatineau. The Gatineau joins the Ottawa opposite the city of that name, the seat of government of Canada. Cameron assured us that the Bos ke-tong and Gatineau were so rapid and broken that no set of men could get a raft down, no matter how well they knew the country, nor how much provisions they might have. He regarded our deliverance as purely providential, and many times remarked that we would certainly have perished but for seeing the smoke from his fire. He was hunting timber for his employers, Gilmour & Co., of Ottawa, and was to start in two days down the Gatineau for his headquaiters at Desert. If we would stay there until he started we were welcome, he said, to food and accommodations, and he would take us down to Desert in his canoe, and at that point we could get Indians to take us farther on. He also said that he had intended to look for timber on Filliman's creek, near where the balloon would be found, as near as we could describe the locality to him, and would try to look it up and make the attempt to get it to Ottawa. This would be a long and tedious operation, as the portages are very numerous between the creek and Desert — something over twenty — one of them three miles long. Over these portages, of coure, the silk must be carried on the backs of Indians.

After eating all I dared to, and duly cautioning LaMountain not to hurt himself by over-indulgence, I laid down to sleep. Before doing so, I had one of the men remove my boots, and when they came off, nearly the whole outer skin peeled off with the stockings. My feet had become parboiled by the continual soakings of four days and nights, and it was fully three months before they were cured.

After finishing up his business in the vicinity were we found him, on Friday morning (our ninth day from home), Cameron started on his return. We stopped, on our way up the creek, at the spot where we had erected our landmark by which to find the balloon. We struck back for the place, and in about twenty minutes found her, impaled on the tops of four smallish spruce trees, and very much torn. LaMountain concluded to abandon her. He took the valve as a memento, and I cut the letters "TIC," which had formed part of her name, and brought the strip of silk home with me. We reached what is known as the "New Farm" on Friday night, and there ended our sleeping on the ground. Up by early dawn, and on again, through the drenching rain, reaching Desert on Saturday evening.

At Desert we were a good deal troubled to obtain Indians to take us further on. LaMab McDougal had told his wife about the balloon, and she, being superstitious and ignorant, had gossipped with the other squaws, and told them the balloon was a "flying devil." As we had travelled in this flying devil, it did not require much of a stretch of Indian credulity to believe that if we were not the Devil's children, we must at least be closely related. In this extremity we appealed to Mr. Backus,* a kind-hearted American trader, who agreed to procure us a complement of redskins, who would take us to Alexis le Beau's place (60 miles down the river), where it was thought we could obtain horses. Sunday morning (our eleventh day from home), we started from Desert, and reached Alexis le Beau's just at night. The scenery upon this part of the route was sublime and imposing. The primeval forest stood as grand and silent as when created. Our Indians, too, surpassed anything I ever beheld, in physical vigor and endurance. In the day's run of sixty miles, there were sixteen portages to be made. On reaching one of these places, they would seize the canoe as quick as we stepped out of it, jerk it out of the water and on to their shoulders in half a minute, and start upon a dog trot as unconcernedly as though bearing no burthen. Arriving at the foot of the portage, they would toss the canoe into the stream, steady it until we were seated, then spring in and paddle away, gliding down the stream like an arrow. In the

---

*Something quite curious grew out of my naming Mr. Henry Backus as having assisted us at the mouth of the Desert river. My account was generally published throughout the country, and some ten days after our return I received a letter from a lady in Massachusetts asking me to describe to her the man Backus, as that was the name of her long-absent son, who, twenty years before, had disappeared from home, and had never afterwards been heard from. I answered the letter immediately, and soon after learned that the man proved to be her son, and that he had promised to come home. What had driven him away from civilization to live among the Indians, was best known to himself. But a man of his generous impulses might have been an ornament to society, and a blessing to his friends. [This note was written the next week after we escaped from the wilderness. The article following this treats of Backus' experience quite exhaustively.]

morning we traveled fifteen miles and made seven portages in one hour and forty minutes.

At Alexis le Beau's we first beheld a vehicle denominated a "buckboard"—a wide, thick plank reaching from one bolster of the wagon to the other, and upon the middle of which plank the seat was placed. This sort of conveyance is often used in new countries, being very cheap, and within the reach of ordinary mechanical skill. Starting off as soon as we could get someting to eat, we travelled all night through the forest, over one of the worst roads ever left unfinished, and reached Brooks' farm, a sort of frontier tavern, in the early morning, where we slept a couple of hours, and after breakfast pressed on by the rough frontier stage towards Ottawa.

While the stage was stopping to-day to change horses, I picked up a newspaper at Her Brittanic Majesty's colonial frontier post-office, and in it read an account of our ascension and positive loss, with a rather flattering obituary notice of myself. And then, for the first time, I began to comprehend the degree of concern of our protracted absence had aroused in the public mind. And if the public felt this concern, what would be the degree of pain experienced by wife, children, parents, friends? These reflections spurred us forward — or rather, our money induced the drivers to hurry up their horses — and at last, on the twelfth day of our absence, at about five o'clock in the afternoon, we jumped off the stage in front of the telegraph office in the good city of Ottawa, whence, in less than five minutes, the swift lightning was speeding a message to home and friends. That was a happy moment — the happiest of all my life — when I knew that within thirty minutes my family would know of my safety.

I do not know how the people of Ottawa so soon found out who we were — but suppose the telegraph operator perhaps told some one, and that "some one" must have told the whole town, for in less than half an hour there was a tearing, excited, happy, inquisitive mass of people in front of the grand hotel there — the clerk of which, when he looked at our ragged clothes and bearded faces, at first thought he "hadn't a single room left," but, who, when he found out that we were the lost balloon men, wanted us to have the whole hotel, free and above board, and had tea and supper and lunch, and "just a little private supper, you know!" following each other in rapid, yet most acceptable succession. The happy crowd in the hotel and upon the street were determined to shake hands with us every one, and nearly all wanted to give or loan us money. Pretty soon the newspaper men and some personal acquaintances began to press through the crowd, and some cried while others laughed and huzzahhed. Indeed, every one acted as if they had just "found something." And such is human nature always, when its noble sympathies are aroused for the suffering or distressed.

Although the president of the Ottawa and Prescott Railroad (Robert Bell, Esq.), volunteered to send us on by a special engine that night, we thought it best (inasmuch as our friends had been informed of our safety), to stay at Ottawa until morning. It did seem as though the generous people of that city could not do enough for us, and their kind attention and disintersted enthusiasm will never be forgotten.

Well, the next morning we left Ottawa, and were quickly carried to Prescott; thence across the St. Lawrence River to Ogdensburg. Here a repetition of the same friendly greetings took place; and at last, after a hearty dinner, we left for home, now distant only seventy-five miles by rail. All along the line of the road we found enthusiastic crowds awaiting our coming, and all seemed to exhibit unmistakeable evidence of the deep interest felt in our fate. At Watertown, which had been my home from boyhood, the enthusiasm had reached fever heat, and the whole town was out to greet the returning aeronauts. They had out the old cannon on the Public Square, and it belched forth the loudest kind of a welcome. My family had, of course, suffered deeply by my absence. Everybody had given us up for dead, except my wife. I felt very cheap about the whole thing, and was quite certain that I had done a very foolish act. Not so the people — they thought it a big thing to have gone through with so much, and yet come out alive.

Several general conclusions and remarks shall terminate this narrative, already too long. "Why did you permit yourselves to go so far?" will naturally be asked. To this inquiry I reply, that the wind was exceedingly light when we ascended; that we were very soon among the clouds, and consequently unable to take cognizance of our course, or to judge how fast we were travelling. It should be distinctly understood that when you are sailing in a balloon, you are unconsious of motion and progress, unless you can see the earth.

Even when you first leave the earth, you seem to be stationary, while the earth appears to drop away from you. Nor can you, when out of sight of the earth, although you may have a compass, judge of the direction you are travelling, if travelling at all. In a few words, *unless you can see the earth, you cannot tell how fast nor in what direction you are travelling.* This, perhaps, better than anything else, will explain why we unconsciously drifted off to latitudes so remote. When we arose above the thick mass of clouds, before sundown, we undoubtedly struck a rapid current that carried us north-east, and after we had travelled in this current about an hour, we probably struck another current, from the variation of our altitude, which bore us off to the north-west, for the place where we landed is about thirty miles west of due north from where we ascended.

When we first descended near the earth, and saw lights and heard dogs barking, we should have landed. But we were unwilling to land at night in a deep wood, even though we knew that inhabitants were near by, and we thought it best to pick out a better place. This was our error; and it came near being a fatal one to us — it was certainly so to the balloon. In trying to find our " better place " to land, we were up longer than we supposed, and as we were travelling in a current that bore us off to the northward at the rate of 100 miles an hour, we soon reached a point beyond the confines of civilization.

La Rue's Treasures.
(The gold seekers of the St. Lawrence. A tale of the Thousand Islands.)

About four miles west of the Mallorytown Landing, on the north shore of the St. Lawrence, at the spot where the original Mallorys first landed, a settler named William La Rue, but commonly known as "Billy" Larue, received a grant of lots 15 and 19, in all, 550 acres of land, in the year of our Lord, 1802. "Billy" was, although eccentric, a man of great energy and endurance. As a proof of the latter quality, it is related of him that he once walked barefooted the whole distance to Cornwall, that being the nearest point at which he could procure sufficient leather for a pair of shoes. At the point where La Rue settled, a deep ravine opened to the river. Across this he managed to construct a dam, thus furnishing himself with a most excellent water power, on which he built a mill, and, in consequence, grew in wealth. During the war of 1812 his mill was taken possession of by the British troops, who utilized it as a means of providing subsistence for the troops.

Although his lands presented almost insuperable barriers to agricultural improvements, Billy persevered in clearing away the original forest, and, in its stead, planted apple, chestnut and walnut trees, so that even now, at a distance of almost a century of time, mingled amongst pines of a second growth, may now and then be found an apple tree, planted by the hand of the original owner of the soil, "Billy" La Rue. But time speed away and Billy toiled on, and as he was never known to be at all profuse in his expenditures, it was surmised that at his death, which was at a good old age, he was possessed of a large amount of gold and silver, which, by constant accretions in the imagination of his acquaintances, grew into fabulous sums which were, of course, buried somewhere on his estate; and though hardly pressed at the time of his death to do so, he died and "made no sign." Having no family, and no heir nor heirs having ever presented a claim to his possessions, the lands, in time, reverted to the State, the mill and dam rotted away, the once cleared lands became covered with a second growth, but the belief in Billy La Rue's buried treasures remained and grew and multiplied more rapidly than did the little groves of second-growth pines which to-day dot the premises, and many have been the excavations made, and many the midnight searches at all points around the house, but so far in vain. While Billy was on his death bed, it was noticed that his fast glazing eyes turned oftenest in a particular direction, and it was along that line of view that the most persistent effort was made; and of one of those midnight searches a record is left by one of the participators, which is given as nearly as possible in his own language.

THE TREASURE-SEEKER'S NARRATIVE.

On a bright moonlight night, in company with three other men, I left the village of Mallorytown and proceeded to a spot in the vicinity of the old La Rue mill near the upper dam. We were provided with a divining rod of witch-hazel, and a goodly supply of picks and shovels, and in fact everything that was necessary to the prosecution of an enterprise of that character. We were in the best of spirits, and as it was a charming night, every way suitable for a successful issue to such an enterprise, we determined, if possible, to unearth Billy's treasures, or at all events to probe the secret to the very bottom.

Our guide was an elderly gentleman who claimed to be an expert in the matter of unearthing buried treasures, and he had carefully instructed in every particular relating to etiquette to be observed on like delicate adventures. One imperative command, I remember well, and that was, that from the moment the divining rod began to indicate the sought for spot, not a word should be spoken, happen what might. We proceeded first to the house and then to the cemetery, at which point we proposed to begin our operations. It was a night of beauty. The moon shone clear and bright through the pines on the overhanging cliff, and yet a feeling something like awe crept over us. Suddenly our leader paused and presented his wand. Slowly the witch-hazel turned toward its mother earth. Moving a few paces to the left, our leader re-adjusted the wand, and again it drooped earthward. Again and again was the mysterious divining rod tested, and always with the same result. That we had solved the secret, and were about to become the happy possessors of the long-buried gold, there was no manner of doubt.

Striking a circle of about twelve feet radius, we began to dig, and so intent were we upon the welcome task that I took no note of the passing time. Whether we dug one hour or six, I cannot tell. Gradually the sky became overcast and one by one the stars disappeared. The moon sank from sight beneath the horizon, while the wind, as it rose in gusts and fell again into a gentle breeze, sighed a mournful requiem among the swaying pines. It grew weird and gloomy, and like a pall darkness came down upon us as we dug, transforming us into spectres in each other's eyes. But we labored on and not a word was spoken.

Next came a blast of icy coldness which chilled the very marrow in our bones, though from our severe exertion we were bathed in perspiration. In the distance we heard a tramping, as of many feet. It seemed as though the guardian spirit of Billy La Rue's treasure was marshalling a force to destroy the desecrators of the last resting place of the dead.

But we were nearing the completion of our labors. Our excavation was cone-like in form, the deepest part being in the center Suddenly a pick struck a metallic substance and the sound rang out clear and distinct on the night air. A few shovelfuls of earth more taken off and we felt the object with our hands ; because of its ringing sound when struck I will always believe it was metal. We redoubled our exertions and rapidly removed the earth from one side and thrust down a crowbar. The coveted treasure was our own. With our united strength we slowly raised the iron covering, when in an instant we were surrounded by creatures innumerable, crowding up to the very edge of our excavation. In the darkness their forms were indistinct, but to judge from the noise of their tramping there must have been thousands of them. They reminded me of a vast drove of black cattle. A great fear which I cannot describe came upon us, and with one impulse we dropped the crowbar and ran for life. Coming out of the ravine near the new mill, we paused. The moon was sailing majestically through a clear sky, though to our belief it had a short time before gone down in gloom. After a brief consultation, we came to the conclusion that we were victims of imagination. We returned to our work. We found our tools and garments, but not a sign of any metallic covering nor even a flat stone at the bottom of our excavation. Our leader sorrowfully shook his head, and declared that the "treasure had moved," and so we departed for Mallorytown, determined to let the treasures of Billy La Rue rest forevermore.

NOTE.—The above story, or the substance of it, was found by the author of this book in an old pamphlet, in which the name of its writer does not appear, else due credit would have been given. It is inserted mainly because its location is among the Thousand Islands.

On Historic Ground.

(From the Congregationalist, Sept. 27, 189,.)

Should an American Walter Scott ever arise he would find ample material for a new series of Waverly novels in the historic associations of the River St. Lawrence and its northern and southern shores. He would find here mighty fortresses built by no human hands, castles made more secure by natural bulwarks than moat or barbican could make them, hidden bays in which a fleet might hide, channels three hundred feet deep winding between wooded islands and secluded water ways. Ellen's Isle, made famous by the Wizard of the North, is reproduced here in a hundred forms, and Loch Katrine has scores of rivals at our very door.

We have our legends of battle and carnage, of valiant deeds by souls as heroic as those who wore the tartan and the plaid. We can point out a cavern hidden away beneath precipitous rock on a secluded island, which has its romance of a maiden's devotion to her father hiding from bitter enemies seeking his life. She, darting through the waters in a little canoe, avoiding the watchful enemy, provided for his needs till the danger had passed. To-day this Devil's Oven, if not as famous as the little island among the Trossachs, is visited by thousands and the heroism of the maiden recalled.

Connected with this act of bravery is the story of her father, William Johnston, as told by one of his old neighbors. About the year 1837 our American steamer Caroline was seized for transporting patriots to Canada and sent over Niagara Falls. In revenge for this act, coupled with real or fancied personal wrongs, Johnston organized a company of frontiersmen, and on Wellesley Island, then almost uninhabited, lay in wait for the new and elegant side-wheel Canadian passenger steamer Peel as it passed down the river to Ogdensburg. It landed for wood at what is now called Peel's Dock. Our informant, then a lad living on a lonely farm, was at the pier to see the great ship. A stranger warned him away, but not far off he saw a little band creeping out from behind huge woodpiles and attack the steamer. The French crew fled into the woods. A few jumped overboard in their night-clothes. The brave engineer sought to scuttle the steamer, but it was fired, drifted out a little way and sank in forty feet of water, where it rests " unto this day."

The night attack on Deerfield, Mass., in 1704, for the rescue of the Bell, and the terrible massacre of Wyoming, were planned on one of these islands. Many of them have their tales of terror connected, with the French and English and Indian wars. No securer place could be found for sudden attacks from hidden enemies in these labyrinthian channels, secluded bays and wooded rocky islands.

The name of Bonaparte is perpetuated by a charming lake not far away. The story of Joseph, the brother of the great Napoleon, and his career in Northern New York is as romantic as any in its history. His coming here to secure an American home for the emperor, after a planned escape from St. Helena, his great domain and elegant chateau, the bringing hither a Venetian gondola to sail on these Western waters, the baronial establishment of retainers and servitors, chariots and outriders, and the royal style in which he lived constitute one of the strange episodes of history. Prior to that time Joseph had been to America, won the heart of one of its brightest maidens, married her — some say a fictitious marriage — carried her to France and placed her in a convent. He promised to take her to court when the opportune time came. That never appeared, as Napoleon had other plans for his brother. At last, with her child, the mock marriage having been made known to her, she fled to Northern New York. A friend saw, in early girlhood, this daughter, in a home where they were both guests. She recalls a stately, queenly woman, bearing a resemblance in face to the noted family.

Not far away, too, is the childhood home of the famous singer Antoinette Sterling, the beauty of whose Christian character has not been exaggerated. Her home is now in London. Many a wild legend do we hear as we glide over these historic waters and listen to enthusiastic informants. As to a cluster of some three hundred islands of special historic interest, a charming poem was a while ago issued in a French newspaper in Quebec, in which this pretty conceit is expressed: "After Adam and Eve had been expelled from Paradise the Garden of Eden was taken back to heaven. On its way thither flowers were thrown back to earth, and these three hundred islands are created from those blossoms of God."   S. E. B.

The Happy Islands.

From proof sheets of Haddock's "Souvenir of the St. Lawrence."

There, where a Thousand Islands sleep,
Come pulsing from Niagara's leap
The blended lakes with tireless sweep —
Vast lakes, which float the grain and ore
Of mighty States from shore to shore,
A thousand billowy miles and more.

'Tis there the centering waters meet
In rush sublime and beauty sweet,
Which we with happy thrills shall greet —
We who in fevered towns have sighed
For green and watery spaces wide,
And Nature's murmuring love beside.

Ah, here they are! The river here,
Swift, slow, tumultuous, crystal-clear,
Lapping the islands which uprear
Their rocky heads, with crests of trees
Has sure enchantments to release
The heart and change its pain to peace.

Hail! River of the Thousand Isles,
Which so enchants and so beguiles
With countless charms and countless wiles;
Flow on unpent, forever free
And pauseless, to the ocean sea
Which belts the globe's immensity.

Not there our goal. Here, here we stay
Among the islands green and gray,
Nor strive, but idly float and play
Along the river's glints and gleams,
And yield to reveries and dreams
With which the quickened fancy teems.

Here, where the airs are always pure,
And wave and earth and sky allure,
And whisper, "Let the best endure,"
The wiser thoughts and instincts grow,
Hearts truer feel and surer know,
And kindle to a tenderer glow.

St. Lawrence River, here we rest,
And here we end our wandering quest
To reach the Islands of the Blest,
Where Nature's sweetest sweets abound,
Are sacred waters, sacred ground —
The Earthly Paradise is found!

GEORGE C. BRAGDON.

GRAND VIEW HOUSE
AND ANNEX COTTAGES,
GRAND VIEW PARK, Thousand Islands, N. Y.

Hourly communication by Steamer. In the center of the Famous Fishing Grounds of the St. Lawrence. Take the Grand View Park Ferry-boat at Thousand Island Park Dock. R., W. & O. R. R. trains connect at Clayton with Steamers landing at T. I. Park. Lake Steamers also land at T. I. Park.

P. O. ADDRESS—GRAND VIEW PARK, (THOUSAND ISLANDS,) N. Y.

Transient Rates, $2.00 to $2.50 per day. Weekly Rates given on application. Special Rates in June and September. Boat Livery connected. Best Bathing Beach among the Islands. Toboggan Slide and Laundry. Address

HAMILTON CHILD, Supt. of Park.

www.ingramcontent.com/pod-product-compliance
Lightning Source LLC
Chambersburg PA
CBHW032241080426
42735CB00008B/951